BARRON'S

SAT®

STRATEGIES FOR STUDENTS WITH LEARNING DISABILITIES

Dr. Toni R. Welkes
Learning Clinician in Special Education and Reading

BARRON'S

All inquiries should be addressed to:
Barron's Educational Series, Inc.
250 Wireless Boulevard
Hauppauge, NY 11788
www.barronseduc.com

ISBN-13: 978–0-7641-3797-6
ISBN-10: 0–7641-3797–2

Library of Congress Catalog No. 2007046828

Library of Congress Cataloging-in-Publication Data

Welkes, Toni R.
    SAT strategies for students with learning disabilities / by Toni R. Welkes.
       p. cm.
    Includes bibliographical references and index.
    ISBN-13: 978-0-7641-3797-6
    ISBN-10: 0-7641-3797-2
    1. SAT (Educational test)—Study guides. 2. Learning disabilities—United States. 3. Learning disabled children—
Education—United States.   I. Title.

    LB2353.57.W475 2008
    378.1'662—dc22

                                                                                    2007046828

PRINTED IN THE UNITED STATES OF AMERICA

9 8 7 6 5 4 3 2 1

Contents

Introduction

CHAPTER 1

LEARNING DISABILITIES EXPLAINED

*My friend, Caitlin, said to me, "You are so lucky. I wish I had extra time to take my tests. I would ace the SAT." She doesn't get it. To me, it's not **extra** time; to me, it's **enough** time. Because of my learning disability, I need more time to read the questions, read all the choices, eliminate choices, and finally pick the one I think is right. I am not getting anything extra. Nobody considers physically disabled people "lucky" when they are given wheelchairs. Why am I considered "lucky" if I am given extended time on a test to help me take it like someone without a learning disability? I wish I could make kids understand.*

Lauren, a 17-year-old high school junior

What are learning disabilities?

The search for a definition of "learning disability" (LD) began earnestly in mid-1960. Around that time, researchers and practitioners began searching for a reason why some children manifested a "gap" between their potential and their performance that could not be attributed to mental retardation, brain injury, or emotional disability. It was hoped that the definition would lead to educational intervention. The research was motivated by the hope that individual education plans could be developed to accommodate the individual differences in learning.

Definitions of "learning disability" have not changed since the federal special education legislation went into effect. In 1977, Public Law 94–142, the federal law that spurred the creation of special education programs in schools across the country, defined "specific learning disability."

"Specific learning disability" means a disorder in one or more of the basic psychological processes involved in understanding or in using language, spoken or written, which may manifest itself in an imperfect ability to listen, think, speak, read, write, spell, or to do mathematical calculations. The term includes such conditions as perceptual handicaps, brain injury, minimal brain dysfunction, dyslexia, and developmental aphasia. The term does not include children who have learning problems which are primarily the result of visual, hearing, or motor handicaps, of mental retardation, of emotional disturbance, or of environmental, cultural, or economic disadvantage.

Federal Register, 1977, p. 65083

According to the Learning Disabilities Association:

A learning disability is a neurological condition that interferes with a person's ability to store, process, or produce information.

Learning disabilities can affect one's ability to read, write, speak, spell, compute math, reason, and also affect a person's attention, memory, coordination, social skills, and emotional maturity.

Common learning disabilities include:

- **Dyslexia**—a language-based disability in which a person has trouble with specific language skills, particularly reading.
- **Dyscalculia**—a mathematical disability in which a person has a difficult time solving arithmetic problems and grasping math concepts.
- **Dysgraphia**—a writing disability in which a person finds it hard to form letters, write within a defined space, and express ideas.

Learning disabilities often run in families.

Learning disabilities should not be confused with other disabilities such as mental retardation, autism, deafness, blindness, and behavioral disorders. None of these conditions are learning disabilities.

Attention disorders, such as Attention Deficit/Hyperactivity Disorder (ADHD) and learning disabilities often occur at the same time, but the two disorders are not the same.

Because learning disabilities cannot be seen, they often go undetected. Recognizing a learning disability is even more difficult because the severity and characteristics vary.

A learning disability can't be cured or fixed; it is a lifelong issue. With the right support and intervention, however, children with learning disabilities can succeed in school and in life.

Learning Disabilities Association of America, 2007

The priority of parents and teachers is not so much the legal definitions of the term "learning disabilities," but more their practical implications observed in the classroom. Legally the term "specific learning disability" indicates a discrepancy between intellectual potential, that is, what we sometimes refer to as I.Q., and performance. In the classroom, a student with a learning disability may require alternate teaching methods to address his or her specific needs. For example, while the average student develops strategies to learn more efficiently, learning disabled students are often unable to develop successful strategies to meet their academic needs. As such, they require direct teaching.

A person classified with learning disabilities

- Can see

- Can hear

- Has intelligence in the near-average to above-average range

- Has problems learning that cannot be associated with poor education or cultural issues *but*

- Cannot acquire and utilize information optimally because of difficulties in perception, language, retention, attention, or motor control

In short, *a learning disability can be any cognitive process that interferes with learning.*

There is a wide range in the types of learning disabilities that students manifest, and, as with physical disabilities, within each type of learning disability, there is a range from mild to moderate to severe. In the past, most states used a discrepancy formula, that is, a formula to assess eligibility for services by comparing the student's potential, as represented by IQ scores, and the student's performance, as represented by the student's achievement scores. However, in recent years, there has been more of a tendency to view the learning-disabled child from the perspective of an alternative learner. In this respect, the student is not viewed as an impaired learner but rather as a "differently-abled" learner. The stigma of deficiency is eliminated, and it is replaced by the view of the student as a positive, strategic learner.

Nevertheless, the classification of learning disabled remains part of the federal law, the Individual with Disabilities Education Act (IDEA), and the student who is legally classified "learning disabled" may be entitled to academic intervention and classroom and/or testing accommodations.

Some examples of testing accommodations or modifications follow:

- *Extended time:* Students may be eligible, based on psychological testing results, to anywhere from 25 to 100 percent additional time.

- *Separate location:* Students may require that classroom standardized tests be administered in an alternative testing room.

- *Reader:* Students whose performance on reading tests indicates a significant deficit in decoding may be eligible to have tests read to them.

- *Scribe or word processor/computer:* Students with severe graphomotor deficits that may manifest themselves in illegible penmanship may be eligible to use a computer/word processor or a scribe to whom they would dictate answers.

- *Enlarged test:* Students with visual perception or processing deficits may be eligible to have their tests enlarged.

- *Record answers in test booklet:* Students with visual perception and/or graphomotor problems may be eligible to record answers in the test booklet rather than on scantron cards or answer sheets.

Remember that students who learn differently are given testing accommodations to enable them to perform at a level where their disability is not acting as a hindrance to their performance. For example, a person with a broken leg is fitted with a cast to walk like a person without an injury. A cast could not be considered an advantage; it is prescriptive. This is the case with accommodations. As Lauren stated about her eligibility for extended time due to her learning disability: "To me, it's not *extra* time; to me, it's *enough* time."

Students with more severe learning disabilities are usually identified early in their school careers and are given appropriate academic intervention. Learning clinicians skilled in special education techniques teach students to apply strategies that frequently consist of structured cognitive methodologies.

Some Types of Learning Disabilities

1. Auditory/visual perception
2. Basic reading(decoding)/reading comprehension
3. Spelling
4. Time/spacial orientation
5. Written expression
6. Interpreting visual data
7. Speech/communication/oral expression
8. Organization/planning
9. Graphomotor control /dysgraphia (handwriting)
10. Long-term memory/short-term memory
11. Sensory integration
12. Mathematics calculation/mathematics reasoning (dyscalculia)

Many aspects of learning and life may be affected by learning disabilities—recall of information, attention span, time, directionality, sensory perception, test anxiety, planning, social skills, study skills, organization, planning, emotional adjustment, just to name a few.

A common characteristic of the learning-disabled student is the "learned helplessness" that frequently develops as a response to the fear of failure. Because of past academic failures, the LD student may be unable to perceive a causal relationship between his/her effort and success. Therefore, when faced with a new task, the student's automatic response is "I can't do it." For example, when a former student, Peter, was given a new test-taking strategy, his knee-jerk response was, "Why should I try it? Nothing ever helped me before."

As mentioned earlier, students with severe learning disabilities that profoundly impact academic progress are frequently identified early in their academic careers, and intervention is begun early. The students with milder disabilities, however, are the ones who are often left undiagnosed far into their academic careers, falling through the so-called "educational cracks."

Who are the students with mild learning disabilities? They are the students whose disabilities may not affect their achievement significantly enough to warrant academic intervention, and so, frequently, they are not identified as being "at risk." These are the students who somehow manage to "get by," although they are unable to perform to their intellectual potential. How do we recognize them?

- This may be the child who, throughout school, places in the low-average range on educational achievement tests and for whom learning is a struggle.

- This may be the child who has independently developed compensatory strategies and an excellent work ethic. As a result, there has been no appreciable or noticeable breakdown in the learning process. Therefore, this child may have superior study skills and exemplary grades, *but* this student must work harder and study longer than his/her peers.

- This may be the child who suffers from extreme test anxiety because of fear of failure.

- This may be the child who dislikes school and is borderline "school phobic."

- This may be the student who has become the "class clown" and adopts an "I don't care" defense against a fear of failure.

As you can see, it is as difficult to identify the typical learning-disabled student as it is to identify all the areas in which learning can break down. However, if a student fails to achieve due to any of the factors described earlier in this chapter, there is a good probability that he or she has a learning disability, and that the learning disability may profoundly impact the student's performance on a high-stakes test such as the SAT.

In addition to the student with learning disabilities, there also exists the "differently-abled" child who may have no specifically defined learning problems but whose learning style may be at odds with the typical teaching methodology. As a result, this child may not learn optimally in the elementary grades, and, as a result, at a later point in his/her academic career, significant gaps may manifest themselves on high-pressure tests such as the SAT. Realistically, the outcome for this "gray-area" student may be the same as it is for the LD student—performance well below potential.

HOW LEARNING DISABILITIES AFFECT GENERAL TEST-TAKING

How do learning disabilities interfere with a student's ability to respond correctly to examination questions?

Parents often blame lack of preparation as the key factor behind poor performance on standardized tests, specifically the SAT. This belief frequently results in family conflicts with parents' accusations of insufficient preparation and teens' denials. However, success on the SAT is not solely a result of preparation. As elementary as it sounds, the ability to respond accurately to test questions is an elaborate, multistep process.

Learning and Test-Taking	
First Step:	Perception of information
Second Step:	Association/link with prior information
Third Step:	Organization and storage in the brain
Fourth Step:	Retrieval of information when a stimulus, such as a test question, appears

The first step in the process is the simple *perception of information*. Once perceived, the information must be associated with previously learned information that is often referred to as *background or prior knowledge*. Assuming that prior knowledge exists, the new information must then be *organized and stored* in the brain. As a final step of the process, when a stimulus appears, as in the form of a test question, the information, properly organized and stored, can be readily *retrieved* from the brain. *The process of learning thus requires perception, association, organization, storage, and retrieval of information.* With a test such as the SAT, however, the process is even more complex because it requires more than mere retrieval of information. This exam measures the ability of the student to *synthesize, manipulate,* and often *evaluate* the information in a transformative process.

Given its complexity, the SAT test-taking process can break down at any point. For example, if a student has poor auditory and/or visual perception, the information intake will be incorrect. Students often state, "But I thought you said. . . ." If the sensory intake or perception of the information is accurate, the information must then be associated and linked to prior information. If the student is unable to generalize information and cannot draw linkages to previously learned information, the new information may be stored in a random, haphazard manner. When the student is called upon to retrieve the information, it may be lost. A breakdown in the learning process at any point may significantly impact student performance.

Problem	Result
• Poor auditory/visual perception	• Inaccurate intake of information
• Inability to generalize or link information to prior knowledge	• Storage of information in a random, haphazard manner
• Random storage of information	• Inability to retrieve information

Learning disabilities and gaps in learning do not disappear; however, their effects can be minimized through the *application of strategies.*

What is a strategy? A *strategy* is the systematic way an individual approaches a given task. This includes the way an individual perceives, plans, implements, and finally, evaluates the task. Most students use strategies, whether they are consciously aware of using them or not. In fact, by the time students have reached high school, many of them have developed a collection of compensatory strategies to help mitigate the impact of their learning disabilities. Students have developed these strategies either independently or through explicit teaching and have found that these strategies helped them improve their academic performance. However, when faced with the anxiety of a high-pressure exam such as the SAT, students may not remember the strategies or may not apply them appropriately. It is no surprise that they may be frustrated and disappointed with the resulting scores. If the strategies students developed throughout their school years cannot help them meet with success on the SAT, what can? The answer may very well be *test-specific strategies.*

What are test-specific strategies for the SAT?

Test-specific strategies are strategies that *specifically* address:

• Critical reading (i.e., reading and sentence completion)

• Math, specifically word problems

• Writing, including grammar

• Test-taking strategies specific to the SAT

Why do test-specific strategies work when strategies the students have used successfully throughout their academic careers fail them?

The answer may lie in the inability of the LD student to generalize learning from one situation to another. In order to understand this, let us examine a high school student, Vanessa, learning similar information in two of her classes, English and U.S. history. In her English class, Vanessa is reading a work of historical fiction set on the Great Plains in the nineteenth century. Her comprehension of the book is demonstrated by her ability to apply critical thinking skills in discussing the plight of the characters trying to survive in an often-hostile environment. Nevertheless, when her U.S. history teacher asks Vanessa questions about the problems faced by pioneers settling on the Great Plains under the Homestead Act, she cannot generalize the information she learned in English and transfer it to another class, in this case, her U.S. history class. Her learning is *situation-specific*; the information absorbed in her English class is not transferred or generalized to the context of her history class. This is often the situation with learning strategies.

To the LD student, strategies are often course-specific and material-specific. *For this reason, the LD student taking the SAT must be presented with strategies that are test-specific.*

HOW STRATEGIC TEST-TAKING CAN HELP

As the time approaches for the LD student to take the SAT, many questions need to be answered.

Is tutoring necessary in order for the student to be successful?

The answer to this question depends on the individual student. Tutoring can occur in the home on a one-to-one basis or in a private or school-based course. If parents should decide on tutoring, it is necessary to research the tutor's or school's record of success as well as their methodology. Does the tutor have experience teaching LD students? What strategies does he or she employ? For example, in the verbal area, does the tutor use the "word list" approach to vocabulary or give students tools to derive meaning from unfamiliar words? Does the school-based course allow for differences in learning styles and previous preparation? Parents need to do their homework.

Is there anything parents can due to minimize test anxiety as the student prepares for the SAT?

Much test anxiety depends on the student's prior experiences and attitudes toward standardized testing in general, and the SAT specifically. Has the student demonstrated test-taking anxiety when faced with standardized testing in the past? If so, it may be necessary for parents to reassure their student that the ability to succeed on the SAT is neither a ticket to the college of their choice nor the key to success in the future. It is merely *one* test, the importance of which has been blown out of proportion. Impress on the student that there are many other deciding factors that college admissions committees consider during the application process, most notably the level of difficulty of course work, class grades, co-curricular and extracurricular activities, and community involvement. However, the reality is that no matter how sincere the parents' efforts to minimize the pressure, students will nevertheless experience anxiety, more so for the LD student who has come to associate standardized tests with failure. That is the reality of the situation.

Nevertheless, it *is* possible for advance preparation to reduce anxiety; if a student feels prepared for the test, he or she may feel more relaxed and less stressed about the testing situation. As such, preparation should include the teaching of test-specific strategies, and the student should have adequate time to practice the strategies and demonstrate visible proficiency with them well before the day of the SAT. In addition, providing the student with standard methods to interpret information through the use of test-taking strategies can make the unpredictable nature of the exam seem predictable, and that will, therefore, help reduce anxiety.

How can this book help the LD student prepare for the SAT?

This book can help the LD student by offering test-specific strategies for the SAT. Although some of the strategies are not original and were not developed solely for the SAT, they were included in this book because of their applicability to the SAT. For example, there are strategies directed at passage-based reading, sentence completion, essay organization and writing, grammar, math, and test-taking, including time management, test anxiety, and practice with the different types of test questions on the SAT. These strategies can provide students with a systematic, structured technique for handling the unknown SAT test questions. With the knowledge that they have these strategies at their disposal, students will feel more confident and more self-assured on the day of testing.

Understand, however, that the focus of this book is to provide constructive test-specific strategies, *not* to teach content. The strategies will help minimize the impact of the learning disability. However, not even test-specific strategies are a substitute for preparation in the academic curricular areas that are tested on the SAT, such as English grammar or math. As a result, this book should be used in conjunction with a comprehensive SAT test-preparation review book such as *Barron's SAT* for optimal preparation.

How should students become familiar with the test-specific strategies?

As mentioned earlier, in terms of the test-specific strategies, the key to successful performance on the SAT is prior exposure to and repeated practice of the test-specific strategies. As part of introducing students to the strategies, it is recommended that parents or teachers model them. Furthermore, during their preparation, students should be encouraged to verbally rehearse the strategies for each test area until they have demonstrated a consistency in initiating them. Basically, the students need to develop *automaticity,* that is, the ability to apply the strategies automatically when they are faced with questions to which the strategies apply. This can be achieved *only* through repeated practice.

The Center for Research on Learning at the University of Kansas has developed an eight-stage instructional process for strategy instruction. They are

- Stage 1: Pretest and Make Commitments

- Stage 2: Describe

- Stage 3: Model

- Stage 4: Verbal Practice

- Stage 5: Controlled Practice

- Stage 6: Advanced Practice

- Stage 7: Posttest and Make Commitments

- Stage 8: Generalization

Although this appears to be a lengthy process, research has revealed that 98 percent of the students who have been taught strategies using this eight-stage instructional method have achieved mastery. Students should not attempt to apply strategies with which they are unfamiliar and for which they do not feel ownership. Testing day is *not* the day to experiment with unfamiliar strategies. Ownership comes from repeated practice, and the test-specific strategies should be practiced and owned *prior* to the test.

Finally, students like Lauren should be made to understand that they can take the SAT multiple times, and, as the expression says, "Practice makes perfect." Thus, as they approach the SAT, students will have the security that comes with advance preparation, the knowledge of test-specific strategies, and the understanding that, should they choose, they will have additional opportunities to improve their scores.

CHAPTER 2

The Critical Reading Section

It's so unfair that I might not get into the college I want because I'm not a good reader. That could affect my whole future. Not being a good reader doesn't mean not being a good thinker. I think colleges don't understand that. You can be smart and just not read well. For example, I watch The History Channel all the time; I mean, just for fun. I watch late night news shows on TV so I keep informed about what's going on in the world. Here I am, seventeen years old, facing the most important test of my life, and I don't know what to do.

Jordan, a 17-year-old senior

HOW LEARNING DISABILITIES AFFECT STUDENT PERFORMANCE IN THE CRITICAL READING SECTION OF THE SAT

Although Jordan's frustration is entirely understandable, his situation is not as bleak as it seems. The problems he anticipates having are not as insurmountable as they appear. This Chapter will discuss various techniques and strategies designed to mitigate the effects of learning disabilities, test anxiety, and poor test-taking.

What problems do learning-disabled students face on the Critical Reading Section of the SAT?

The Critical Reading Section is a challenging section of the SAT for most students; for students with learning disabilities, particularly with a deficit in the area of reading comprehension, it can be especially demanding. The reading passages are lengthy, intellectually demanding, frequently boring, and often frustrating. Why do LD students have particular problems in this area of the exam?

- LD students tend to be *weak in the language-based skills* upon which the exam draws.

- Vocabulary is featured prominently as a necessary skill, and students who *lack an extensive vocabulary* have a disadvantage in the sentence completions, the passage-based reading, and even the directions and language of test questions. Moreover, since reading is one of the single most important factors in vocabulary growth, LD students are often at a disadvantage in this section because many LD students do not read sufficiently for vocabulary enrichment.

- In addition to the knowledge of vocabulary, the *nuance of language*—semantic differences, syntactic variations, and pragmatic use of language—is also being tested in the Critical Reading Section.

- Many learning-disabled students possess an *inadequate fund of background knowledge* because of insufficient reading or reading on a narrow range of subjects. Therefore, their ability to activate prior knowledge in order to interact with the text and construct meaning is restricted.

- Many LD students fail to read at the *level of difficulty* at which the passages are written.

- Psychological factors such as *fear of failure* and *test anxiety* may present obstacles to student performance on the Critical Reading section.

- Students with *problems sustaining attention* may find the complex sentence structure, the passage length, and uninteresting subject matter in the passage-based reading tedious and frustrating.

- Students may *lack efficient test-taking and time management strategies.*

Problems LD Students Face on the Critical Reading Section

Task	Problems Faced by LD Students
Vocabulary	• The level of vocabulary is too difficult.
	• Students fail to understand degrees of difference in word meanings.
Fluency	• To construct meaning, students must be able to read fluently.
Decoding	• Students may have difficulty decoding technical or foreign words.
Reading Comprehension	• Students possess little prior knowledge of subject matter.
	• The reading level of the passage is too difficult for the student.
	• The sentences are long and have multiple clauses.
	• Students have few or inadequate comprehension strategies.
Other Factors	• Students have problems sustaining attention.
	• Students may lack confidence and fear failure causing test anxiety.
	• Students may have problems with time management.

Since the ability to comprehend is crucial to reading success and, therefore, to success on the Critical Reading Section of the SAT, it is important to understand what is involved in reading and comprehending. According to the National Reading Panel (2000), good readers use *three types of strategies*:

1. *Pre-reading strategies,* in which students bring background information to the reading task
2. *During reading strategies,* in which students monitor their understanding of the reading task
3. *Postreading strategies,* in which students reflect on whether they understood the reading task to the nature of comprehension

It is important to understand how the issue of *prior knowledge* is crucial. When there is some prior knowledge of the reading topic, the student is able to make associations that will mitigate the difficulty of the reading task. For example, having seen a movie about knights, the student will have some background knowledge about the feudal system and may be able to visualize a castle, a moat, armor, jousting, and possibly even the chivalric code. This will provide some background information on which readers may draw. However, students with attention deficit disorder who have studied the feudal system in school may or may not have given the subject their full attention and so will not have sufficient background information. In addition, students with long-term memory or retrieval problems may be unable to make the necessary associations in order to access the background information they require.

What additional factors impact the performance of LD students on the Critical Reading Section of the SAT?

TASK DIRECTIONS

Even though the task directions may be confusing, they are fairly standardized; therefore, students can prepare themselves in advance for the requirements of the task. For example, the directions preceding the passage-based reading states:

> *The passages below are followed by questions based on their content; questions following a pair of related passages may also be based on the relationship between the paired passages. Answer the questions on the basis of what is stated or implied in the passages and in any introductory material that may be provided.*

What are the directions asking the student to do? Examining each clause individually, the directions state that

1. The questions following the passage will be based on their content, or what the passage contains.
2. When there are two related passages, the questions may involve the relationship between the two passages.
3. The answer to the questions should be based on the information stated or implied in the passages.
4. The answer may also be based on any introductory information provided.

Once the student has broken down the directions into the component tasks and understands what is required of the passage-based reading tasks, there will be no surprises concerning the requirements. Therefore, *preparation is essential* in order for the student to feel comfortable with the task directions.

MULTIPLE-CHOICE QUESTIONS

Students are unable to prepare in advance for the multiple-choice questions associated with the passage-based reading, and the language and sentence structure of the questions and the choices may be challenging. (See Chapter 5 for strategies concerning multiple-choice questions.)

The following is an example of a question that may confuse students:

> *In context, the description in lines 18–26 of Shirley McGinnis's way of conversing with her neighbors suggests the narrator's belief that her personality reflects . . . .*

The student is asked to perform *three* evaluative tasks in the course of one question:

- *Refer* to a conversation appearing in specific lines in the text

- *Explore* the subject, Shirley McGinnis's style of conversation, in the context of the passage

- *Assess* how the conversation reflects Shirley McGinnis's personality

Under the constraints of time and the anxiety associated with the SAT, it is understandable how many students can find the task of interpreting multiple-choice questions formidable.

VARIATION IN QUESTION TYPE

Passage-based reading questions may vary from those requiring *literal information* that can be found directly within the text, to those requiring extended reasoning or *inferential interpretation*. The latter type of question requires students not only to process information but to draw conclusions and make judgments about what they have read. Thus, this type of interpretive reading measures the students' ability to synthesize and analyze information that they have processed in the passage.

For example, most adults can recall elementary school reading comprehension tasks of the type, "Mary wore a red dress. What color was the dress that Mary wore?" This is an example of literal interpretation. The answer can be found directly in the passage. However, contrast this with the inferential question, "Why did Mary wear a red dress to school?" This requires a student not only to comprehend the literal meaning but to assess how wearing a red dress may be symbolic.

Students taking the SAT may come across a variety of critical reading tasks, such as finding the main idea, making predictions, determining cause and effect, drawing conclusions, sequencing information, defining contextual vocabulary, recognizing author's tone, and analyzing characters. Once again, the SAT is examining students' abilities to interpret and evaluate what they read as reflective of the higher level reading tasks that they will presumably encounter in college.

The *order of the questions* themselves may often confuse students as they vary from the concrete to the abstract with, for example, a concrete question like "The meaning of the word *fortuitous* in line 16 means . . ." can be followed by an inferential question like "You can infer from the passage, that the relationship between Kevin and his cousin, Harley, ..." The questions in the Sentence Completions and Math sections of the SAT are arranged in ascending order of difficulty so that students can gauge whether to answer some of the later questions. However, since there is no logical progression of difficulty in the questions following the reading passages, the student is often confused by the random quality by which very difficult and very easy questions, as well as concrete and abstract questions, are interspersed.

Concrete Question: "The 'friend' referred to in line 17 most probably refers to . . . ." A question of this nature requires only that a student locate the line and determine the information requested.

Inferential Question: "The comparison stated in lines 18–25 suggests the author's belief that fictional characters . . . ." A question of this nature requires the student to synthesize the information in the passage, evaluate it, and make a judgment of the author's position based upon the information.

TIME MANAGEMENT

In addition to the nature of the passage-based reading task itself, many other problems may arise for the learning-disabled student in the Critical Reading Section of the SAT. One such issue is *time management*. Although many LD students have extended time as a test modification, they nevertheless may be uncertain as to how to manage their time, extended or not, on a lengthy test such as the SAT. Knowing the importance of the test results, many students will often labor at questions they should omit, wasting time that could best be applied toward questions that they are capable of answering correctly. It must be kept in mind that the SAT is a "penalty test," in which 1/4 of a point is deducted for each incorrect response. For this reason, it is *not* in the student's best interest to answer every question. Students need to make determinations as to which questions to answer and which to omit. Test-taking strategies will be discussed further in Chapter 5.

TEST ANXIETY

Finally, there is the issue of test anxiety. As success promotes success, often failure, or the fear of failure, promotes the fear of additional failure. Conditioned by early lack of success, the anticipation of failure often causes students to "freeze up" causing a *cognitive paralysis* where the students are unable to recall information or make even basic connections between ideas. Under those circumstances, higher order thinking becomes impossible.

In addition, as a result of test anxiety, many students may demonstrate *uncharacteristic test-taking behavior*. For example, the student may become "stuck" on a question or a reading passage and be unable to progress through the rest of the test. Similarly, anxious students may experience "memory meltdowns," where, in response to each test question, they return to the passage, reading and rereading it. With test anxiety, as with time management, many students require strategies to help them relax, focus, and advance their way through the exam. See Chapter 5 for strategies to help students manage test anxiety.

These are just a few of the problems many students with learning disabilities face in the Critical Reading Section. Some issues that are inherent in this section of the exam and that affect student achievement go beyond the critical reading skills themselves. The most proficient reader may break down under conditions of anxiety and pressure. Because optimal performance on the Critical Reading Section of the SAT requires a variety of skills and strategies, it is difficult to establish a single area upon which to focus. Therefore, the student with learning disabilities may require multiple test-specific strategies in order to maximize success on the Critical Reading Section.

VOCABULARY STRATEGIES

Word knowledge has long been recognized as an indicator of comprehension, so it comes as no surprise that a thorough knowledge of vocabulary is at the heart of the Critical Reading Section of the exam and is assessed both in the sentence completion and the passage-based reading areas.

As a result of this emphasis on vocabulary, many teachers involved in test preparation have students memorize lengthy word lists. How successful is this strategy for the student with learning disabilities? Learning lists of words out of context is *not* an effective strategy for *any* student!

Why *don't* word lists work for LD students?

• Requiring students to recall extensive lists of noncontextualized words, that is, words out of context, under conditions of test anxiety will only intensify test anxiety.

• Many students with learning disabilities have difficulty retaining and retrieving information, and the stress may be heightened when they are asked to recall lists of words.

• The SAT does not merely require students to recall definitions; the students are asked to apply higher order thinking skills, that is, application and problem-solving, to demonstrate their knowledge of word meaning.

Why are LD students at a disadvantage in acquiring vocabulary?

Poor Reading Comprehension: Students who do not understand what they are reading will not retain any unfamiliar vocabulary they encounter because these words are not meaningful to them. In addition, many LD students tend to avoid reading as much as possible because they find it so tedious. As a result, these students have few opportunities to build new vocabulary.

Poor Decoding: The student with poor decoding, that is, word attack skills, may likewise avoid reading because just making sense of the written word is a frustrating task. In addition, the effort of "sounding out" words interferes with fluency and, thus, comprehension. As a result, what cannot be understood cannot be recalled, and the ability to remember vocabulary is impaired. Whether the cause of the reading disability is poor decoding, lack of word recognition, insufficient sight vocabulary, or reading comprehension problems, the result is the same—deficient reading vocabulary.

Poor Listening Comprehension: Reading is not the only vehicle by which students learn new vocabulary; many students learn by hearing unfamiliar words spoken in the context of conversation. However, listening comprehension is problematic for LD students with language processing or attention problems as evidenced by the poor oral vocabularies many such students possess, and therefore these students may require additional strategies for building vocabulary.

In an effort to increase students' acquisition of new vocabulary in the lower grades, some language arts teachers had students interrupt their reading to look up unfamiliar words in the dictionary, causing an aversion to both reading and the dictionary. Other teachers required students to make flash cards with unfamiliar words and then memorize their meanings. The new vocabulary words were filed in students' short-term memory, accessed for tests, and often promptly forgotten if they were not applied.

What works?

The key, then, in acquiring new vocabulary is application. Once students use a new word, they assume ownership of that word, and they can be reasonably expected to both identify and apply that word in the future without overtaxing their retrieval ability.

Thus, rather than rote memorization, it is more efficient to have students

1. **View** words in their context
2. **Link** the words with already-known words
3. **Practice** applying the words

How, then, do students acquire new vocabulary without memorizing lists of words?

WORD SUBSTITUTION

It has long been understood that students acquire vocabulary from the context in which it appears. While test preparation is taking place for the SAT, students are simultaneously involved in their coursework at school. Therefore, while doing required reading in their high school classes, students should take note of unfamiliar words. If they encounter new vocabulary in their content area reading or in the course of reading literature, they should *substitute a word* that "fits" into the context and then write the unknown word on a pad or a sheet of paper alongside the substituted word. What the students need to determine is how close their substituted word comes to the unknown word in order to calculate a *guess ratio*.

For example, in the sentence: "Academic skill is viewed as a kind of *virtuosity*, much like musical ability, and is thought to be of value to the student who is intellectually gifted." The student, unfamiliar with the word "virtuosity," substitutes the word "talent." The question, "In line 17, the word *virtuosity* as it appears in the sentence means (a) desire; (b) reward; (c) key; (d) note; (e) aptitude." The student then looks among the choices for a synonym of the word "talent." Looking at the contextual clue, "much like musical ability," specifically the word "ability," the student eliminates choice (a) because desire is not a talent or ability; eliminates choice (b) because a reward is a gift given to somebody for an achievement, not something innate as a talent or ability; eliminates choice (c) as being too much of a stretch in meaning; eliminates choice (d) as being irrelevant; and finally, the student is left with the correct answer, choice (e).

What happens if the student makes an incorrect substitution? In the sentence, "In most Western countries, the university is endowed with political and economic influence of *gargantuan* proportions." Let us assume that the student has substituted the word, "intellectual." Looking at the choices, (a) destructive; (b) unusual; (c) enormous; (d) inverse; (e) insignificant, it becomes apparent that there is no synonym for the student's choice, "intellectual." Therefore, it is obviously incorrect. Thus, in order to determine the guess ratio, the student must calculate how many substitutions are accurate and how many are inaccurate.

How to Establish a Guess Ratio During Reading

- During reading, note unfamiliar vocabulary.

- Substitute a familiar word that "fits" into the context.

- Write the unknown word on a piece of paper.

- After the reading is concluded, look up the unfamiliar word in a dictionary.

- Determine how close the substituted word is to the original unknown word.

- Chart the ratio of times the substituted (guessed) word and unknown word are synonyms.

This method also enables the students to *measure their own comprehension*. If the substituted word is fairly close in meaning to the definition of the unknown word after several attempts at substitution, in other words, if the guess ratio is high, then students can rely fairly comfortably on their ability to establish the contextual meaning of new vocabulary. However, if the students find that their substitution of words in context is inaccurate after a number of such attempts, in other words, if their guess ratio is low, they need to consider other vocabulary strategies.

What if the student shows a high ratio of successful substitution of familiar words for unknown vocabulary in context? How do students go about *establishing ownership* of the new vocabulary? The student then needs to make a conscious effort to use the new word (1) when speaking and (2) when writing. Usage is the *only* way by which students learn vocabulary. They assume ownership as they manipulate language to communicate and share ideas. In addition, it is through usage that students learn the nuances of meaning, and often, it is these nuances, the degrees of difference between words, that are explored on exams such as the SAT.

If students do not have many reading demands in their courses, and this occurs frequently in a technology-driven curriculum, they must create reading experiences. A good source of unfamiliar vocabulary is a quality newspaper or news magazine. Here students can acquire the conceptual or abstract vocabulary that is most commonly found on exams such as the SAT.

LISTENING

In the case of students with learning disabilities, vocabulary is acquired more frequently by listening than by reading. For many students with reading problems, reading is a time-consuming, arduous task. These students tend to use their auditory, or listening, mode as their primary learning channel and are able to absorb vocabulary by hearing words used contextually, perhaps by listening to the radio or watching television. However, the new words will be forgotten if students do not take ownership of the new word. As mentioned earlier, in order to own a word, students must recall the context in which the word was spoken, and, they should use the new words in the course of their own discussions.

For example, if students hear two political opponents discussing deficit spending, they should attempt to follow the exchange and derive as much meaning as they are able. Next, they should explain each candidate's point of view to their parents, siblings, or friends, and possibly write a statement of the candidates' positions using the new vocabulary.

In addition, students who prefer listening to reading may also exercise the option of listening to good quality, perhaps classic, books on tape; however the exposure, the students must make an effort to determine the meaning of unfamiliar words in context. As with students who have acquired new vocabulary through reading, those who have learned new words through listening can ensure retention through the ownership that is claimed by repeated usage.

STRUCTURAL ANALYSIS

Another vocabulary strategy that enables students to access the meanings of unfamiliar words is affix acquisition, otherwise known as *structural analysis*. Although the technique of learning affixes, that is, word parts such as prefixes, roots, and suffixes, is not new, its effectiveness has been substantiated. Most students examining the internal structure of words by focusing on prefixes, suffixes, and roots will not only improve their knowledge base of word meanings but will actually improve their decoding, or ability to "sound out," unfamiliar words. Even if students do not gain the full definition of an unfamiliar word but only the ability to categorize the word, they have a tool with which to attempt an answer.

For example, by studying the prefix *mal-* (bad), the student is able to place words such as "malediction," "maladroit," "malefactor," and "malady" in a class of words that denote something "bad" or negative. As a result of learning just this one affix, the student has acquired a comprehension tool that can be applied to many previously unknown words. As a result of studying structural analysis, the student is able to make connections between previously acquired vocabulary and the unfamiliar words encountered on the SAT. (See Appendix A for a list of prefixes, suffixes, and roots.)

SPLIT-PAGE STRATEGY

An effective strategy to use in teaching students through structural analysis is the *split-page strategy* (see Figure 1). In a notebook designated for vocabulary acquisition, have students:

- Fold a sheet of paper in half lengthwise so the left side of the page faces up

- Write an affix such as the above-mentioned *mal-* on the side facing up

- Write all the words containing that affix on the right side, the side facing down, with their definitions

- Check recall of vocabulary by a frequent review of the prefixes, suffixes, and roots

Word Part	Examples
mal- (bad, wrong)	Malfunction, malformation, malevolent, malcontent, maladapted, maladroit, malady, malediction, malefactor, malfeasance, malicious, malign, malignant

Figure 1: Example of the Split-Page Strategy

In addition, using this strategy, students with learning disabilities are able to maximize their learning through *classifying and sorting information* into categories because retrieval, or the recall of information, is facilitated when information is organized in the brain. Thus, using a split page format as shown in Figure 1, students could make a list with examples of negative prefixes such as *non-, un-, ir-, mis-, mal-, anti-*. In this way, students are at least able to classify words as negative even if the exact definition is unknown. This can be an important tool when applied to sentence completions as well. By having students draw connections between words with similar affixes (prefixes and suffixes), their need to recall an exact word meaning is minimized as is their test anxiety.

KEYWORD STRATEGY

A strategy that has been successful with many students who have learning disabilities is the *keyword approach* (Pressley, Levin, & MacDaniel, 1987). This strategy is of greatest utility to the student who not only has a problem *learning* new word meanings but, in addition, has problems *remembering* the meanings. In this strategy, an unknown word or, rather, a word to be learned, is paired with a familiar word, called a *keyword,* that sounds or looks like part of the unknown word. The keyword is then linked through words or a pictorial representation to the original or unknown word. This connection between the keyword and the unknown word now enables the student to retrieve or remember the meaning.

For example, let us assume the unknown word is "monkeyshine," meaning a prank. The pictorial representation could be a monkey shining a flashlight into the face of a sleeping lion. Thus, the connection is being made between the definition of monkeyshine, that is, a prank, and the pictorial, a monkey shining a flashlight into the face of the sleeping lion. In this manner, the student is then able to retrieve the definition "prank" by recalling the picture of the monkey. The keyword strategy enables students to improve their understanding of factual and content-specific terminology, remember new vocabulary, retain word meanings for a longer period of time, and improve application of word meaning. Because this technique is student-directed and student-generated, it is, therefore, enjoyable for students to use.

How to Use the Keyword Strategy

1. **Pair** the unknown word with a familiar word (the keyword).
2. **Link** the keyword to the unknown word through a word or a picture. *Hint:* The more ridiculous the word or picture is, the easier the word will be to remember.
3. **Use** the link between the keyword and the word/picture to recall the meaning of the unknown word.

MOTOR IMAGING STRATEGY

For students with a kinesthetic learning style, that is, whose learning is facilitated by movement, *motor imaging* (Casale, 1985) may prove to be a successful approach to vocabulary acquisition because it enables the student to use multiple modalities: the visual, by reading the word; the auditory, by saying the word; and the kinesthetic, by using arm motions. With the motor imaging approach, the student pairs a new vocabulary word with a gesture that describes it. For example, the new vocabulary word, "undulate," meaning wavelike motion, could be accompanied by a rising-and-falling motion of the hand indicating a wave; the vocabulary word, "facile," meaning easy, could be accompanied by a snap of the fingers; and the vocabulary word, "pliable," meaning flexible, could be accompanied by stretching an imaginary substance. These are merely a few examples of how motor imaging could be utilized as a method of vocabulary acquisition, application, and recall.

How to Use the Motor Imaging Approach

1. **Read** the vocabulary word to be acquired.
2. **Say** the word aloud.
3. **Pair** the word with an arm or hand motion that describes it. For example, for the vocabulary word, "supplicate," the hands might be put together in a gesture of prayer.
4. **Use** the gesture to recall the vocabulary word.

THE SCANR STRATEGY

When students encounter an unfamiliar word during their reading, they are usually encouraged to substitute the word, "blank," and continue reading, thus attempting to derive the meaning of the unknown word from its context. The *SCANR Strategy* provides students with a mnemonic that breaks down the process of acquiring meaning from context into a series of steps, with each letter representing a step in the process. According to this strategy, students would *substitute* a word(s) for the unknown word. Next, they would *check* to see if the context supports their substituted word. To verify that it does, they would *ask* themselves if, in fact, the context clues support their substitution. If the clues do not, students would *need* a new idea and would then have to *revise* their word.

For example, Mary encounters the sentence: "In an effort to stem the flow of illegal drugs into our country, the government is increasing border security guards." Mary knows what the word "stem" means as a part of a plant, but not in the context of this sentence. However, as she reads the sentence with "blank" in place of "stem," she understands from the context of the sentence that the government perceives drugs flowing into the country as a problem. Therefore, Mary *substitutes* "stop" for the word "stem." Next, Mary *checks* the sentence to see if the context supports her substituted word. "In an effort to stop the flow of illegal drugs into our country, the government is increasing border security guards." Mary would then *ask*, "Does the sentence make sense with the word 'stop' substituted?" The answer is yes. However, if Mary, thinking of "stem" as something that goes up from associating "stem" with a plant, substituted the word "increase," she would see that the context of the sentence does not support her substituted word. Why would the government increase the border security guards if they want more drugs flowing into the country? Or, for that matter, why would the government want to increase the flow of drugs into the country? In either case, Mary would *need* to come up with a new idea for the meaning of "stem" and then *revise* her word.

The SCANR Strategy

- **Substitute** a word(s) for the unknown word.

- **Check** the context for clues that support it.

- **Ask** if the substitution fits all the context clues.

- **Need** a new idea?

- **Revise** the substituted word to fit the context clues.

To maximize vocabulary acquisition, application, and recall students require

- A rich exposure to vocabulary through good quality listening or reading material

- An understanding of how words are used in sentences, or their syntax, as well as how the words are used in different contexts

- Methods to retrieve word meaning without overtaxing their memory and creating additional anxiety

- Multiple exposures to a new word

- Multiple opportunities to develop ownership of the word

- A familiarity with prefixes, suffixes, and word roots, that is, structural analysis, to enable them to gain a general meaning of unfamiliar words

Because there is a wide variety in the individual needs of language-learners, students need to pay careful attention when selecting the appropriate strategies. Whatever strategy or strategies students choose; the goal remains the same—vocabulary acquisition, application, and recall.

Application of Strategy

1. After an exhaustive search of the house, the police concluded nothing had been stolen.

   In the line above, "exhaustive" most nearly means

   (A) tired
   (B) successful
   (C) thorough
   (D) destructive
   (E) random

2. Archaeologists unearthed clues about the aboriginal people of Bora Bora.

    In the line above, "aboriginal" means

    (A) first
    (B) abortive
    (C) sun worshipping
    (D) martial
    (E) winsome

3. The bibliophile spent his entire vacation alone with his classics.

    In the line above, "bibliophile" means

    (A) recluse
    (B) liberator
    (C) lawyer
    (D) book lover
    (E) doctor

4. The two boys, accused of fighting, claimed as a defense that it was just horseplay.

    In the line above, "horseplay" means

    (A) gambling
    (B) jumping
    (C) racing
    (D) stealing
    (E) rough play

5. The doctor warned me that the medication could cause somnolence.

    In the line above, "somnolence" means

    (A) dizziness
    (B) sleepiness
    (C) sadness
    (D) sickness
    (E) awareness

Answers and Applications of Strategies

1. *Answer:* (C)

    Strategy applied: Using the word substitution strategy, the student would substitute a word that fits the context of the sentence. Using the context, the police are conducting a search and coming to the conclusion that nothing was stolen. What kind of search would reveal that information? The student might substitute the word "careful." Using the student's substituted word, choice (a) makes little sense but leads to the erroneous conclusion that "exhaustive" and "exhausting" must mean the same. Choice (b) makes no sense in the context of the sentence. Choice (e) random could not be the answer because a random search would not lead to a conclusion. Choice (d), while seemingly a possible choice, is not quite as good a choice as the answer.

2. *Answer:* (A)

   Strategy applied: As in Question 1, choice (b) was included to draw attention to the fact that its first four letters were the same as "aboriginal." In fact, the two words are unrelated in meaning. Using structural analysis, students can identify the root, *mart* meaning "warlike," and eliminate choice (d). Similarly, identifying the root" *orig*, meaning "beginning" in the word "aboriginal," students can conclude the correct answer is choice (a).

3. *Answer:* (D)

   Strategy applied: Using structural analysis, the students can identify *biblio* as "book" and *phil* as "love" and arrive at choice (d).

4. *Answer:* (E)

   Strategy applied: Because "horseplay" does not lend itself to structural analysis, the student may wish to use either the word substitution strategy or the keyword strategy. Using the latter, the student could draw a picture of a horse playing football, and standing atop a football player. A pictorial representation such as this can easily prompt the recall of the definition, "rough play."

5. *Answer:* (B)

   Strategy applied: Using the motor imaging strategy, the student could pair the word "somnolence" with the action of "yawning," indicating sleepiness. In this way, the student could recall the meaning.

SENTENCE COMPLETION STRATEGIES

Students with learning disabilities will probably benefit from strategies in this section of the SAT because of the nature of the sentence completion task. By way of comparison, this section is similar to a puzzle in which all the pieces are present but need to be put together in a logical, coherent way; however, the good news is there are clues to help students decipher the puzzle. That is where the strategies come in; they facilitate the students' understanding of the clues.

The Sentence Completion Section is almost mathematical in its logic. Sentence completions can be compared to deductive reasoning exercises in which one must use the information given to eliminate choices until an eventual solution is reached. In the Sentence Completion Section, students are provided with numerous semantic and punctuation clues since the word omissions occur within a context. Therefore, there is a compelling reason for students to learn and apply strategies to sentence completions: They provide the means to decipher the clues. Many LD students may have problems eliminating choices because of their limited vocabulary. For this reason they need to depend on the above-mentioned clues.

Before examining the strategies themselves, the student should *picture the sentence as a mathematical equation* in which words and punctuation help "balance" the sentence. For example, one part of the sentence may have a negative bias. Depending on the connecting words, or conjunctions, the rest of the sentence may continue in the same way, or the meaning of the sentence could shift to a positive bias. This connecting word is the clue that will signal the student to select a word from among the choices that is either positive or negative. When students examine sentences from this perspective, they are able to apply simple logic to offset their limited vocabulary.

In addition, they are able to use the clues in the sentence along with the balancing technique to maximize their vocabulary.

Semantic Strategies

Semantic clues are those that apply to *word meaning*. For example, morphemic or structural analysis of words is included as a semantic clue. Using the meanings of affixes (prefixes and suffixes) and roots of words assists the student in selecting or eliminating choices in a Sentence Completion exercise. (See Appendix A for a listing of prefixes, suffixes, and root words.)

There are many ways this can be done. One way is to examine the prefix of a word for a clue as to the bias of the word, that is, whether it is positive, negative, or neutral. For example, the prefix *pro-*, *bene-*, and *philo-* may indicate that the word is positive, and the prefixes *non-*, *un-*, *im-*, *in-*, and *mal-* may indicate that the word is negative. This is important to know if a student is trying to balance a sentence and is not sure of the meaning of a word.

The sentences may have *one or two blanks*. Regardless of the number of blanks, students must remember to insert the word "blank" when they read it for the first time. In this way, they are preserving the flow of the sentence so the context may provide valuable clues as to the missing words.

Although it would appear as though the sentence completion with one blank would be easier for a student, this is not always the case. While there are rarely multiple clauses to confuse the student in the one-blank sentence, there may also be fewer clues provided. The strategies are somewhat different for the one-blank sentence and the two-blank sentence.

In the **one blank-sentence**, the student must

- *Focus on the subject* of the sentence because often the only clue to the answer comes from an understanding of the relationship of the subject to the blank

- *Substitute* a familiar word in the blank

For example, in the sentence, "The professor considered it his mission to _____ knowledge to his students," the first step would be to identify the subject of the sentence—the professor. Using the student's background information, what mental image would come to mind? The picture in the student's mind might be of a professor, or teacher, standing in front of a class giving a lecture. What is the mission, or purpose, of the professor? The professor's purpose may be to educate his students. However, it makes no sense to substitute the word "educate" in the context of the sentence where it would precede the word "knowledge." One cannot educate knowledge. Nevertheless, one can transfer, transmit, provide, spread, promote, or give knowledge. Therefore, substituting any of the above words, which would most probably be a part of the student's vocabulary, and examining the choices, (a) apply; (b) explain; (c) disseminate; (d) extricate; (e) elucidate, it would appear that choice (c) would make the most sense.

In applying these strategies, the student has effectively accomplished *three important aims*:

1. The student has *identified the subject* and used his or her own background knowledge to get a mental image of that subject, both of which would help greatly in analyzing the sentence.

2. The student has *taken ownership* of the sentence by substituting a word that makes sense in the context of the sentence.
3. The student has developed the means to *monitor comprehension* of the sentence because the student knows that if a synonym or a word similar to the word substituted is not among the choices provided, he or she has failed to comprehend the sentence correctly. Under those circumstances, the student knows to return to the sentence and reread it for another possible meaning.

Utilizing students' background knowledge in order to enable them to substitute a familiar word into the context of the sentence is a powerful method of deriving meaning from sentences and maximizing success in performing sentence completions, particularly sentences containing one blank.

Where there are *two blanks*, the student could, of course, substitute a familiar word in each blank as with the one-blank sentence; however, the student is likely to achieve greater success applying other strategies. One of the most important semantic strategies a student can apply is that of "balancing" a sentence by paying close attention to *connecting words or conjunctions*. To understand how this works, examine a common descriptive phrase "tall, dark, and handsome." For the most part, "tall" is considered a positive attribute. The same is true of "dark." Having seen two positive attributes followed by the word "and," one expects another positive attribute. In this way, the word "and" performs a similar function as an equal sign, that is, positive plus positive equals positive (i.e., positive + positive = positive). Looking at the sentence from this perspective, the word *"and" indicates no shift in meaning* from positive to negative.

As proof of this, it is unlikely for somebody to be referred to as "tall, dark, and strange" or "tall, dark, and unattractive." The characteristics are not necessarily mutually exclusive, and it is certainly possible to possess the first two positive attributes alongside the negative third attribute; however, it is uncommon to find descriptions written this way. They are far more likely to read, "He was tall, dark, but unattractive." In this case, the word *"but" indicates a shift in meaning* from positive to negative.

EXAMPLES

He was tall *(+)*, dark *(+)*, and *(=)* handsome *(+)*.
He was tall *(+)*, dark *(+)*, but *(shift in meaning)* unattractive *(–)*.

So conditioned are people to the word "but" indicating a change from positive to negative, that they anticipate what will follow upon hearing it. For example, "Pearson, you are a good worker but . . ." or "Diane, you are my best friend but . . ." or "Johnny, you may borrow the car tonight, but. . . ." In all the above instances, the conclusion of the sentence was omitted because the reader could furnish the sentence completion based on the shift in meaning implied by the word "but."

There are several other connecting words that demonstrate either continuity or change, or, if you will, an equal sign or unequal sign. The word "although" usually indicates a shift in meaning. For example, the reader of the clause, "Although Anna is my best friend . . ." can make an assumption that what follows will contrast with the idea of Anna as a "best friend." Words like "despite" and "in spite of" also indicate a shift from the expected. For example, "Despite the fact that the sky was dark and cloudy in the morning, the weather was beautiful and sunny in the afternoon." This sentence challenges readers to change their ideas and acknowledge an alternative possibility. The word "yet" also indicates an idea that does not flow logically from what preceded it. For example, "Carol had no real talent, yet she became famous."

In some sentences, a causal relationship is indicated so that the reader is presented with an idea that flows naturally from the one preceding it. Words like "since," "because," "when," "if," and "so" indicate such a meaning. For example, "When Janet realized neighbors could look into her living room, she hung curtains." The second part of the sentence is a logical action stemming from the first part of the sentence. Looking at another example, "Because John was unsuccessful as a coach, he returned to teaching," the reader can anticipate that John would have to choose an alternative occupation after reading the first half of the sentence. Conjunctive adverbs such as "thus," "consequently," "moreover," and "therefore" indicate continuity. The words "whereas" and "however" usually indicate shifts in meaning.

Thus, the key to success in the *two-blank sentence* is to

- *Establish* what is required in the first blank and then take particular note of the connecting words to determine whether the second part of the sentence is proceeding in the same direction as the first or an altered direction.

- *Apply* structural analysis strategy by examining prefixes, suffixes, and roots for clues that will allow students to eliminate obviously incorrect choices and possibly take an educated guess.

Words Indicating a Connection in Meaning

- and

- too

- also

- in addition

- similarly

- besides

- moreover

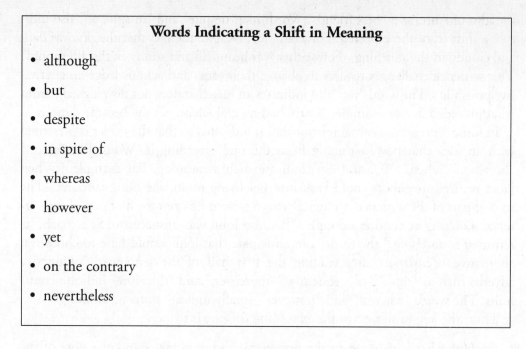

Words Indicating a Shift in Meaning

- although
- but
- despite
- in spite of
- whereas
- however
- yet
- on the contrary
- nevertheless

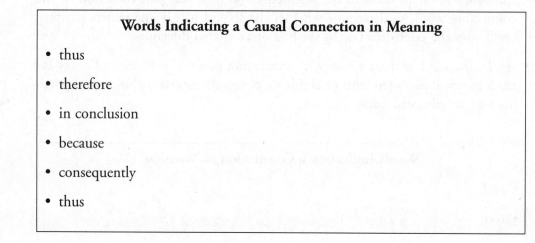

Words Indicating a Causal Connection in Meaning

- thus
- therefore
- in conclusion
- because
- consequently
- thus

PUNCTUATION STRATEGIES

Most students view punctuation as necessary to set off quotes, separate clauses, and differentiate between a question and a statement. Few see *punctuation as a possible guide to meaning*. However, punctuation can be a valuable tool to help a student understand the relationship of one part of a sentence to the other.

Students trained to see the sentence as a balanced equation, can draw a parallel between commas and the word "and" in a series. If "and" indicates parallel meaning, the comma performs the same function.

However, a comma can also alert the reader to a shift in meaning. For example, "I will stop by your house on the way to school, but don't expect me to wait if you are late." The comma forces the reader to pause and take note of the change in direction. In addition, the comma can emphasize the conjunctive adverbs such as "however," "consequently," "thus," and "therefore" when they appear in the middle of the sentence. For example, "Sue failed the test and, therefore, felt that she had not studied hard enough." However, a comma, *except when substituted for the word "and," is not* a reliable clue to meaning; rather it highlights words that can be important clues to meaning.

A punctuation mark that gives a clue to continuity in meaning is the semicolon. Semicolons link two independent clauses that are closely related in meaning. For example, "My mother was never good with plants; she once killed a plastic plant." One can infer that what follows the semicolon will be similar in meaning to what has preceded it. Therefore, if there are two blanks in clauses separated by semicolons, students can reasonably assume that there will be no shift in meaning from positive to negative or vice versa. Paying attention to the use of semicolons is a good strategy for students trying to maximize their understanding of the direction in which sentences are going.

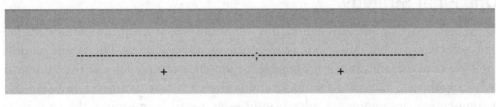

Figure 1

Colons can have a variety of functions. They can be used to introduce a long or a formal list, and they can introduce a quotation. However, there are times when the use of a colon is a signal that a word, phrase, or sentence will explain, magnify, or summarize what is being said. When a colon is used in this way, what follows the colon explains what preceded it. For example, "As a chef and a husband, Alex knew the ingredients that would improve any relationship: chocolate and love." Thus, the use of the colon in an explanatory manner can assist a student to understand the continuity in a sentence.

Punctuation Indicating Continuity of Meaning

- commas (in a series)

- semicolon

- colon

The ENTER Strategy

To summarize the steps to answering sentence completions, students should recall the ENTER Strategy. In this strategy, students examine the sentence filling in the word "blank" when one appears in order to get the general direction and flow of meaning. Next, students *note the words and punctuation clues* that will provide them with hints as to how to balance the sentence. Once that has been done, and students are aware of the direction of the sentence, the next step is for them to *try to fill in a word or words* of their own that make sense in the given context of the sentence. When students have done this, they need to then *enter a choice* that is similar in meaning to their own word or words and makes sense. In the case of the two-blank sentence, both words must apply. Having done this, students need to *recheck for meaning*.

The ENTER Strategy

Examine the sentence.

Note word and punctuation clues.

Try to fill in a word or words based on meaning.

Enter a choice that makes sense.

Recheck for meaning.

One Final Strategy

In the Sentence Completion Section, it is important that students do *not* look for the one correct answer but rather look to *eliminate the wrong answers.* This is true of most multiple-choice exams, but it is essential for sentence completions. If the student is balancing the two clauses of a sentence and is given a positive word in one clause and a conjunction or conjunctive adverb indicating a shift in meaning, the student is looking to insert a negative word in the second clause. To do so effectively, the student will need to eliminate any choices that could be construed as positive.

For example, "In the morning, John jumped up, eager to face the day, a study in _____, but, by late afternoon, he was a study in _____." (a) exhaustion . . . energy; (b) focus . . . banality; (c) excitement . . . vigor; (d) momentum . . . inertia; (e) impairment . . . lucidity.

In the above example, the student must examine the first clause for meaning. The clue is that John "jumped up." John would not "jump" if he were suffering from exhaustion or impairment. Therefore, choice (a) and choice (e) can be eliminated. The word "but" indicates a shift in meaning. If John is active as indicated by his jumping up in the first part of the sentence, the student can look for John to be somewhat inactive in the second part of the sentence. That would eliminate choice (c). Most students would know the meaning of the word "focus," and would therefore correctly eliminate that choice as having no relevance to the sentence. By getting a mental picture of somebody awakening, eager to face the day, and, after noting the connector, juxtaposing the image with that of somebody dragging themselves around, the student is able to get a clear idea of both the incorrect choices to be eliminated and the correct choice.

The level of difficulty of the sentence completions ranges from 1, the easiest questions, to 5, the most difficult questions. The questions are arranged in *ascending order of difficulty,* that is, the easier questions are first and they become more difficult as the student moves on; as a rule, the first column questions are generally easier than the second column questions. For that reason, students should definitely answer the first one or two questions, try to answer the next two or three questions, and be very skeptical about the rest. Much has been said about background information and prior knowledge. If, after reading a sentence completion, students have little or no understanding of what the sentence requires, they should not attempt to answer it. *An incorrect answer means a one-quarter point deduction from the total of correct answers.*

Here is one other hint that students may want to apply to the Sentence Completion Section—when there are two words choices that are opposite in meaning, one of them is frequently the answer. Therefore, if students are unsure as to the answer, they may want to scan the choices for a hint. However, *this strategy should be applied with caution* since it is not true 100 percent of the time.

To Be Successful on the Sentence Completion Section, Students Must

- **Use** mental imagery
- **Substitute** familiar words
- **Apply** logic
- **Pay attention to** semantic and punctuation clues
- **Use** the ENTER Strategy

Application of Strategies

1. While house hunting, the Smiths carefully checked beachfront homes because recent storms _____ the coast.

    (A) expanded
    (B) improved
    (C) shielded
    (D) eroded
    (E) cancelled

2. Hawaii's _____ has caused it to preserve its unique culture and traditions.

    (A) natural resources
    (B) isolation
    (C) beauty
    (D) closeness
    (E) volcanoes

3. E-mail has _____ communication; messages are now sent and received instantaneously.

    (A) prioritized
    (B) created
    (C) revolutionized
    (D) hampered
    (E) detained

4. Thomas Jefferson was a _____ statesman, architect, and president, but his personal behavior has _____ his professional accomplishments.

    (A) competent . . . discredited
    (B) qualified . . . glorified
    (C) mediocre . . . magnified
    (D) superior . . . established
    (E) limited . . . devalued

5. Countries of the Middle East would do well to try _____ to resolve their differences; compromise might pave the way to a lasting _____.

   (A) aggression ... understanding
   (B) violence ... upheaval
   (C) communication ... hostility
   (D) friendship ... apathy
   (E) negotiation ... peace

Answers and Applications of Strategies

1. *Answer:* (D)
   Answer Explained: Reading the sentence for meaning, the key words are "beach-front," "storms," and "coast." Using word substitution as a strategy, students might substitute "wore away," and, looking for a synonym among the choices, they would choose "eroded."

2. *Answer:* (B)
   Answer Explained: The key in this sentence is "preserve its unique culture." If students had no idea of the answer, the opposites "isolation" and "closeness" could provide a hint. Students could then ask themselves, "Which would cause a society to 'preserve its unique culture and traditions'?" The answer would lie in "isolation" from other societies rather than "closeness."

3. *Answer:* (C)
   Answer Explained: Taking a clue from the semicolon, which indicates no shift in meaning, students can conclude from the fact that "messages are now sent and received instantaneously," that e-mail has changed communication. Looking for a synonym for "changed," they would find "revolutionized."

4. *Answer:* (A)
   Answer Explained: The word "but" used in the above sentence indicates a shift in meaning. Therefore, if the first part of the sentence is positive, the second part would be negative; if the first part were negative, the second part would be positive. Looking among the choices, students would detect a shift in meaning in choices (a) and (c). Using prior knowledge of Jefferson's accomplishments, which were certainly more than mediocre, students would be drawn to (a) as the correct choice.

5. *Answer:* (E)
   Answer Explained: The presence of a semicolon indicates no shift in meaning between what precedes and what follows the punctuation. Therefore, if the first part of the sentence is positive, the second part will also be positive; if the first part is negative, the second part will be negative. Students could then eliminate choices (a), (c), and (d), which have shifts in meaning. In choices (b) and (e), there are no shifts in meaning; however, students will need to focus on the key word "compromise," as well as to call upon their prior knowledge of the Middle East to look to the positive choices as opposed to the negative.

PASSAGE-BASED READING STRATEGIES

The purpose of this section is to maximize the learning disabled student's score on the passage-based reading by minimizing the impact of the learning disability through the application of strategies. In order to accomplish this, it is necessary to examine how the LD student's critical reading skills may be compromised by the combined impact of the disability and test anxiety.

What problems do LD students have with passage-based reading?

• Reading level of passage may exceed student's reading ability.

• Multiple-clause sentences may obscure meaning of passage.

• Vocabulary level may be too high.

• Student may have no background knowledge about subject of passage.

• Passages may be overly long and boring.

Given any or all of these factors, students *must*

1. **Read** carefully
2. **Focus** complete attention
3. **Be aware** of the intricacies of figurative or technical language
4. **Use** stated facts to draw conclusions or interpret meaning
5. **Retain** important information

However, these tasks appear daunting when coupled with time constraints and the pressure that accompanies knowledge of the importance of the SAT.

What are the strategies LD students can apply to enable them to achieve success on this section of the exam?

Potential Problem: **Test anxiety**
Solution: **Relaxation strategies**
   The student should practice a few relaxation strategies before beginning to read. Whether these involve meditation, deep breathing, or sequential muscle relaxation is immaterial; anything that can help the student reduce anxiety is a crucial first step. (Further relaxation strategies are found in Chapter 5.)

Potential Problem: **Difficult test directions**
Possible Solution: **Prior exposure to directions**
   Having relaxed somewhat, the student must then turn his or her attention to the directions. The familiarity with the directions that comes from good test preparation should enable the student to relax further. Realistically, there should be nothing incomprehensible in the directions since the student has become familiar with them through repeated exposure.

Potential Problem: **Reading rate and time management**
Possible Solution: **Previewing test questions**

Having read through the directions, the student should turn his or her attention to the questions. Reading the questions prior to reading the passage may activate recall of the student's prior knowledge and background information. Having advance information about the topic of the passage may also prepare the student for the requirements of the reading task. The method of reading a highly scientific passage is clearly different from that of reading a literary piece. The objectivity of one passage versus the subjectivity of the other may require that different perspectives be brought to the reading task, and the students need to preview the topic in order to properly focus attention and bring previously learned information to the reading situation.

In addition, the student needs to adjust his or her reading rates according to the type of passage being read. Competent readers automatically adjust their reading rates according to the level of difficulty of the reading task. Many students with learning disabilities are unable to align the task and their reading rates; they will read an article in a teen magazine at the same rate as a scientific essay. Therefore, a pre-examination of exam questions may be helpful in creating a mindset for a technical passage or artistic passage. Furthermore, scanning questions in advance will enable the student to underline unfamiliar vocabulary or unfamiliar word usage, which may then be clarified upon reading the passage.

Potential Problem: **Specific versus global questions**
Possible Solution: **"W" or "P" strategy**

Following a general examination of the questions, the student must next determine whether the individual questions concern the *whole* reading passage or a *part* of the passage and indicate this with a marginal notation, either a "W" or a "P." There is a clear reason for making this distinction before reading the passage; many students focus on the final sentences of a reading passage, finding it difficult to distance themselves sufficiently in order to view the passage holistically. As a result, when asked questions concerning the best title or main idea, questions obviously based on an understanding of the entire passage, the students look at details contained in the last paragraph and, therefore, respond incorrectly. By assessing the aim of the questions in advance of answering them, the student can then respond to the "P" questions first. Having answered "P" questions about vocabulary in context or a specific item of information, the student's perspective of the entire passage is gradually restored, and the student can then respond to global questions.

Possible Problem: **Retention of information**
Possible Solution: **Marginal notations; highlighting**

Having determined in advance the information required by the questions and having a purpose for the reading (that is, to answer the specific questions), the student can then focus on the passage itself. Many LD students, particularly those with retrieval problems, cannot rely on memory strategies alone to retain information from the passages. The reading passage may be too difficult and the test-taking anxiety too intense. Therefore, the student must forego reliance on memory by making **marginal notations** about the reading. The notations can explain a word in context or indicate the antecedent of a pronoun. They can indicate the mood, relate the author's purpose, or explain a convoluted phrase. If the student wishes to add background information for the purpose of making the passage easier to understand, this is acceptable. In addition, the student may learn from the advance examination of the questions that specific information is contained in, for example, lines 6 through 13. In that case, the student may choose to **highlight words or phrases** in these lines that indicate the correct response. By making marginal notes and highlighting significant information, the student is reading actively rather than passively and, as a result, is relying less on the memory of what has been read. In addition, marginal notes enable the student to scan the reading passage quickly for relevant information. It minimizes the amount of time spent rereading the passage and is, therefore, an effective time-management strategy.

Potential Problem: **Monitoring reading comprehension**
Possible Solution: **Tracking main ideas and details; reader-author dialogue**

During the reading, it is important for the student to track the main ideas of the individual paragraphs as well as the supporting details. In this way, the student is constantly differentiating between major concepts and minor details and is engaging in an ongoing process of evaluation. Key ideas should be underlined and, once again, marginal notations should be made.

In addition, as the student reads, he or she should question the information in the passage, rather like having a running dialogue with the author. This enables the student not just to predict what is likely to occur but also to *monitor comprehension*; the student will not be able to ask or answer questions if the text is too difficult. At that point, the student needs to determine what, if anything, he or she has understood, and then to make explanatory marginal notes to that effect. For students with attentional deficits, responding to the passage is also an excellent method of staying focused; if attention wanders, the student would be unable to respond to the passage.

Potential Problem: **Insufficient or inaccurate reading comprehension**
Possible Solution: **Review of passage**

It is a natural tendency, on completion of the passage-based reading, for the student to proceed directly to the questions, but the student needs to resist this temptation and review the passage, once again *self-questioning* for comprehension. Following this review, however, students must return to the questions.

Potential Problem: **Inability to engage with text of passage**
Possible Solution: **TWA Strategy**

The TWA Strategy (Mason, 2004; Mason et al., 2006), Think before reading, think While reading, think After reading, was designed to help reading comprehension through student engagement with the text before, during, and after their reading. The "T" step contains three components for activating students' prior knowledge; the "W" step contains three components that target students' reading behavior; and the "A" step contains three components that enable students to reflect on what they have read.

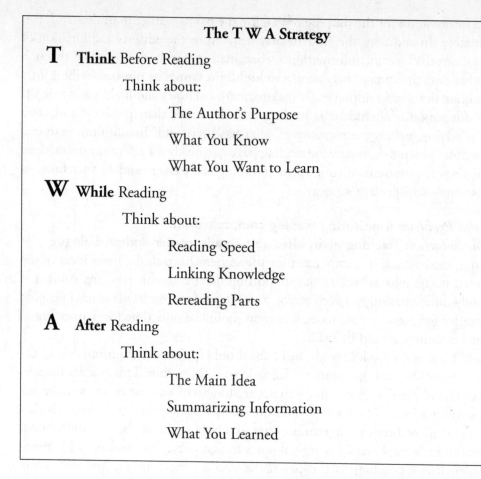

The T W A Strategy

T **Think** Before Reading

    Think about:

        The Author's Purpose

        What You Know

        What You Want to Learn

W **While** Reading

    Think about:

        Reading Speed

        Linking Knowledge

        Rereading Parts

A **After** Reading

    Think about:

        The Main Idea

        Summarizing Information

        What You Learned

TWA Graphic Organizer

Main Idea	
Detail	
Detail	
Detail	

Main Idea	
Detail	
Detail	
Detail	

Main Idea	
Detail	
Detail	
Detail	

Potential Problem: **Impulsive responses**
Possible Solution: **Elimination strategies**

As stated above, the first questions to be addressed will be those dealing with specific parts of the passage and calling for explicit information (i.e., vocabulary in context, literal information, or even inferential information limited to a specific location within the passage). The student should *never* look for the correct answer but rather look to eliminate incorrect answers. LD students, especially students with attentional problems, tend to select the first or second choice because "it sounds right." One review of the tests of LD students, particularly those with attentional problems revealed most, if not all, of the selected choices to have been (a) or (b). The practice of eliminating incorrect choices forces students to focus their attention on *all* the choices.

Another approach that enables students to eliminate choices involves examination of the words of the questions themselves. Words such as "always," "never," "none," "all," "every," and "each" indicate choices that are rarely, if ever, correct because they indicate absolutes. Instead, students should look at choices that contain words such as "sometimes," "usually," "several," "many," or even "most" because these choices present realistic qualifications.

Finally, after completing the "P" or part questions and upon returning to the "W" or whole-passage questions, the student must remember that the correct responses must be *applicable to the entire passage*. Questions concerning the main idea should be expressed in broad terms. If there is any paragraph that fails to relate to the choice, it is incorrect. Similarly, titles should be all-inclusive. If a proposed title relates only to some of the paragraphs of the passage but not others, it should not be selected as the correct choice.

To summarize, students should

- *Eliminate* the incorrect answers (rather than look for the correct answers).

- *Eliminate* choices containing absolute words (e.g., "never," "always").

- *Eliminate* main idea or title questions that relate to only a part of the passage.

As with all sections of the exam, students should resist the temptation of changing answers *unless* they have misread the question or they feel completely certain that their answer is incorrect. It is much more important to spend time relating to the passage, that is, *making marginal notes, underlining key concepts*, and *noting background information* on the topic, than to review answers. This caution is important and bears repeating: Students should *not* change their answers unless they are completely certain that they are changing an incorrect response to a correct one.

Potential Problem: **Answering too many questions**
Possible Solution: **Educated guess, or 50/50 strategy**

The next issue for discussion concerning the passage-based reading refers to the omission of answers. Should students omit answers? If so, under what circumstances? Remember that this is a penalty test; that is, one-quarter of a point is deducted from the correct total for each incorrect answer. Unlike the Sentence Completion Section where the difficulty level is progressive so that the student can logically assume that the early questions will be easier than those that occur later in the section, the passage-based reading questions are interspersed; an "easy" question asking for specific information that can be easily located within the passage may follow an abstruse, interpretive question. Therefore, if after attempting to apply the above strategies, the student is still unable to comprehend the passage sufficiently to narrow choices significantly enough to make a so-called educated or 50/50 guess, it might be wise to omit the question. A reading passage usually contains no more than five or six questions, and the overall impact on the total score of so few omitted questions will not be overwhelming. Therefore, it is not worth the time or anxiety for students to labor over a passage that makes no sense to them.

Potential Problem: **Loss of attention and focus**
Possible Solution: **Medial summary strategy**

Unlike the Sentence Completion section of the SAT, the passage-based reading gives few if any clues. The most effective tool is the student's ability to focus. The student who finds his or her mind wandering during the reading of a lengthy, uninteresting passage should refocus. A strategy for refocusing is the *medial summary*. After one or two paragraphs, the student should make a short marginal summary of what he or she has read.

The student would also be wise to attempt the longer passages with more questions while still somewhat refreshed. There are two reasons for this:

1. The student's perceptions will be sharper and more insightful when he or she is alert, and
2. It is best to complete the longer passages when the student's ability to attend to them is optimal because there are more points to be gained by them.

Therefore, the longer passages should be attempted first, while the shorter passages with fewer questions should be left for last.

Potential Problem: **Inability to understand organization of information**
Possible Solution: **Graphic organizer**

In some cases, students are overwhelmed by the length and concentration of information provided in the reading selections. When this occurs, the student may have difficulty following the organization of the paragraph. Thus, the ability to differentiate between main ideas and details is seriously compromised. In this case, the *use of a graphic organizer* to enable visualization of paragraph organization could be a valuable tool. For example, the organizer shown in Figure 2 allows students to prioritize main ideas and details concerning the topic of the individual paragraphs within the selection as well as determine the relationship of the paragraphs to each other *and* the main topic of the selection. (This and other specific graphic organizers can be found at *www.enchantedlearning.com/graphicorganizers/.*)

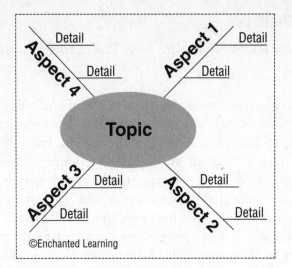

Figure 2: Graphic Organizer

Strategies for Passage-Based Reading

- **Use** relaxation techniques to alleviate test anxiety

- **Attempt** longer passages before shorter passages

- **Read** questions before reading the passage

- **Mark** questions "P" or "W" (part or whole)

- **Read** passage

- **Make** medial summaries

- **Write** marginal notes

- **Underline** words or phrases as needed to answer questions

- **Eliminate** incorrect choices

- **Omit** questions when choices cannot be reduced to two

- **Create** a graphic organizer to prioritize information within and among paragraphs

---

The key to maximizing performance on the passage-based reading is to *preview* the passages and questions, *underline* key words and make marginal notes, *monitor* attention by making medial summaries, *answer* questions pertaining to part of the paragraph before attempting whole-paragraph questions, ***read*** all choices carefully, and *eliminate* incorrect choices. By focusing on specific reading strategies to address the Critical Reading Section of the SAT, students like Jordan, whose frustration was evident in the introduction to this chapter, would feel more positive about his performance.

Application of Strategies

The following passage is adapted from the book, The Uprooted, *a study of immigrants, by Oscar Handlin.*

1   Loneliness, separation from the community of the village, and despair at
2   the insignificance of their own human abilities, these were the elements that, in
3   America, colored the peasants' view of their world. From the depths of a dark
4   pessimism, they looked up at a frustrating universe ruled by haphazard,
5   capricious forces. Without the capacity to control or influence these forces
6   men could but rarely gratify their hopes or wills. Their most passionate desires
7   were doomed to failure; their lives were those of the feeble little birds which
8   hawks attack, which lose strength from want of food, and which, at last
9   surrendering to the savage blasts of the careless elements, flutter unnoticed to
10   the waiting earth.

11   Sadness was the tone of life, and death and disaster no strangers.
12   Outsiders would not understand the familiarity with death who had not daily
13   met it in the close quarters of the steerage; nor would they comprehend the
14   riotous Paddy funerals who had no insight of the release death brought. The
15   end of life was an end to hopeless striving, to ceaseless pain, and to the
16   endless succession of disappointments. There was a leaden grief for the ones
17   who went; yet the tomb was only the final parting in the long series of
18   separations that started back at the village crossroads.

19   In this world man can only be resigned. Illness takes a child away; from
20   the shaft they bring a father's crippled body; sudden fire eats up a block of
21   flimsy shanties, leaves half of each family living. There is no energy for
22   prolonged mourning. Things are as they are and must remain so. Resist not
23   but submit to fortune and seek safety by holding on.

1. This passage serves mainly to discuss the

    (A) death of an immigrant child
    (B) immigrant funerals
    (C) harshness of immigrant life
    (D) family lives of immigrants

2. In line 19, the word "resigned" means

    (A) depressed
    (B) hardworking
    (C) frustrated
    (D) accepting

3. In comparing the immigrants to the "feeble little birds which . . . flutter
    unnoticed to the waiting earth" (lines 7–9), the author is implying that the
    immigrants are

    (A) unimportant
    (B) sick
    (C) winged
    (D) weak

4. The word "steerage" in line 13 means

    (A) the room from which the ship is navigated
    (B) living quarters for poor passengers
    (C) the dining area of the ship
    (D) the deck of the ship

5. The author's tone is

    (A) angry
    (B) sad
    (C) proud
    (D) objective

6. The frustration the immigrants feel in the first paragraph is caused by

    (A) loneliness
    (B) hunger
    (C) lack of control
    (D) sadness

Answers and Strategies Applied

Note: Prior to answering the questions, the student should decide which questions apply to the whole passage and which to a part. Those that apply to specific lines or words should be answered first; that is, questions 2, 3, 4, and 6. Having done so, the student is now ready to examine the questions pertaining to the whole passage.

1. *Answer:* (C)
   Strategy Explained: The only answer that refers to all parts of the passage is choice (c). The death of the child, the funerals, and the family life are all characterized by and indicative of the harshness of immigrant lives.

2. *Answer:* (D)
   Strategy Explained: During the reading of the passage, the student is underlining important words. In this question, the word to note is "only." Man can have reactions other than depression (e.g., bitterness or loneliness). "Only" also eliminates hardworking. In light of what the immigrants are experiencing, "frustrated" does not appear descriptive enough. If students were substituting their own word or words, they would insert words indicating "putting up with" or "tolerating." The dual strategies to be used in a question of this type are, first, to eliminate choices and, second, to attempt a substitution of a familiar word.

3. *Answer:* (A)
   Strategy Explained: The first step is to eliminate choice (c). "Winged" is irrelevant: immigrants are not winged. The passage mentions illness, but the specific lines do not, so choice (b) can be eliminated. Although the word "feeble" may allude to the birds being weak, the two lines taken in their entirety point out how "unnoticed," and therefore how unimportant, the immigrants are. The best strategies to use in this question are underlining, the elimination of choices, and an examination of the word to be defined in the context of the entire quote.

4. *Answer:* (B)

   Strategy Explained: Once again, the student has most likely underlined the essential words preceding and, perhaps following, the word to be defined. As a result, "familiarity with death . . . in the close quarters of steerage" would be highlighted, and would eliminate choice (a), since rooms from which ships are navigated are seldom considered crowded or "close quarters." The same is true for dining rooms and decks. Thus, focusing on the highlighted words and eliminating all choices that do not apply would be the best strategy for students answering a question such as this.

5. *Answer:* (D)

   Strategy Explained: In this passage, the student, having pre-read the questions, should be prepared to write marginal notes indicating the author's tone. Choice (c) is easily eliminated because at no point in the passage is the author's tone "proud." There is no indication of anger in the author's tone, so choice (a) can be eliminated. The student must be careful not to confuse the author's tone with the line, "Sadness was the tone of life." Choice (b) can be eliminated. A reading of the passage reveals the author's restraint as he states the plight of the immigrants in an *objective* manner.

6. *Answer:* (C)

   Strategy Explained: As suggested, students need to pre-read the questions. In doing so, they will be reading the first paragraph to determine the cause of the immigrants' frustration and highlighting key words and phrases. Even though "loneliness" was cited as a factor that "colored the peasants' view of their world" and "want of food" (hunger) and "despair" were also cited as problems facing the immigrants, the notion of lack of control is repeated throughout the paragraph. For example, the immigrants were described as feeling "the insignificance of their own human abilities," and "they looked up at a frustrating universe ruled by haphazard, capricious forces. Without the capacity to control or influence these forces." If the student highlighted these words, the answer would become readily apparent.

Therefore, pre-reading and highlighting are effective strategies in helping the student to locate the correct answer when all choices appear probable.

By focusing on specific reading strategies to address the Critical Reading Section of the SAT, students like Jordan, whose frustration was evident in the introduction to this chapter, would feel more positive about their performance.

Writing Strategies

Writing was never a problem for me. I used to love writing stories and poems in school. When the ideas were in my head, writing was easy. Now it's so hard for me. My teachers and my parents say that I don't study enough. That's not true! The facts are there; I mean, in my head. I read the question, and I know what to say, but somehow between knowing what to say and getting the words out on paper, that's where my problem is. I learned how to write an essay in English. I know the things I have to know about topic sentences, and all that stuff; it's just that, when it comes to sitting down and writing, it all flies out of my head. I can sit with a blank piece of paper or a computer screen—it doesn't matter which—and nothing, just nothing, comes out. It's gotten so that when I know I have to write an essay, I freeze up inside knowing that I'm going to have trouble.

Peter, a 16-year-old junior

HOW LEARNING DISABILITIES AFFECT STUDENT PERFORMANCE IN THE WRITING SECTION OF THE SAT

Unfortunately, Peter's problem and his resulting frustration are common among *all* students, those with learning disabilities and those without. Most adults can recall an incident at some point in their own education when they were under pressure to produce a piece of writing and found they were unable to do so. In this chapter, students will be introduced to some structured organizational strategies that will help alleviate some of the anxieties students like Peter face when writing.

If we look at the communication skills—speaking, listening, reading, and writing—as being related, we will see that listening and reading skills involve receptive language, since both are used to take in information, while speaking and writing involve expressive language, since both transmit information. Examining speaking and writing skills, or oral and written expression, we see that both involve the

1. Motivation to communicate
2. Organization of information
3. Transmission of information

This chapter will break down the skills required on the writing section and give students strategies to help them meet with success.

What skills are required for success on the Writing Section of the SAT?

- Mechanical skills (i.e., capitalization, punctuation, spelling; word order, sentence construction, and paragraph construction)

- Handwriting and/or computer literacy

- Vocabulary

- Reading comprehension

- Development of a theme and/or thesis

- Knowledge of essay writing, specifically persuasive essay writing

In short, students need to plan, organize, carry out, and revise a persuasive essay while keeping in mind vocabulary and language appropriate to audience as well as the conventions, or mechanics, of standard written English. In addition, on the Identifying Sentence Errors, Improving Sentences, and Improving Paragraphs components of the Writing Section, students will be responsible for identifying and correcting errors in standard written English.

What problems do LD students face on the Writing Section of the SAT?

Students face problems on the Writing Section because many of them have difficulty

- Generating ideas in response to the task, often because they cannot comprehend the writing prompt

- Organizing ideas

- Prioritizing ideas and/or seeing a relationship between similar ideas

- Expressing ideas due to insufficient vocabulary

- Understanding and using idiomatic and/or figurative language

- Knowing the mechanical aspects of written expression (i.e., subject-verb agreement, verb tenses, sentence construction, punctuation, spelling)

- Expressing ideas in writing due to negative past experiences or insufficient experience

In an effort to support the students like Peter with writing problems, this chapter will break down the writing task and present strategies for the various components.

WRITTEN EXPRESSION STRATEGIES

Before beginning to address the writing task, the student must understand the purpose of the SAT essay. Briefly, the student is to take a position on the given topic and write an organized essay defending this position; the essay is, therefore, essentially a position paper.

At the start of the 25-minute essay, the student will read a brief essay prompt. The prompt contains general statements. Beneath the box containing the prompt is the assignment, or specific task, the student is expected to fulfill. This is often phrased as a question, the answer to which is the student's position or thesis.

What steps are involved in the writing process? A good strategy for examining the writing task holistically is the *TOPIC Strategy*.

The TOPIC Strategy

The TOPIC Strategy enables the student to see the sequence of steps necessary to perform the required persuasive essay or position paper. By the mnemonic "TOPIC," the student will recall that the first step required in writing the essay is to *take a position*, agreeing or disagreeing, with the proposition stated in the essay prompt. This is perhaps the most important step since the rest of the essay will flow from the student's opinion. To formulate a position, the student must first carefully examine the language of the prompt, self-question what the task is asking, and then reread the question. Remember, the student should *never* attempt to defend both sides of an issue, simultaneously agreeing and disagreeing. First of all, it makes the student appear indecisive. Second, it doubles the student's burden to present evidence substantiating both sides of an issue.

Next, the student must *open the essay* in such a way that the reader is able to understand exactly what position the student has taken. This requires a thesis statement that is precise in directing the essay in the direction the student wishes it to take. The thesis statement has been compared to a gun: if aimed properly, the essay will follow. Therefore, much thought needs to go into the thesis statement.

Just as an attorney attempts to convince a jury of his client's innocence through the skilled use of evidence, so the student must *persuade* the reader of the credibility of the student's position. Knowing that the task involves persuasion, the student must utilize any and all accumulated background information as evidence. To effectively persuade the reader, the student must *insert examples, experiences, quotations, data, or historical information*. Unfortunately, because the student will not have knowledge of the task prior to the exam, the task of planning the essay before the actual writing is critical to its success.

When all evidence has been presented to convince the reader of the validity of the student's viewpoint, the final step is for the student to *close the essay strongly*. To do this, the conclusion should reiterate the most significant points that were made in the essay, preferably in order from the least important to the most important points.

The TOPIC Strategy

Take a position

Open strongly

Persuade your audience

Insert examples/personal evidence

Conclude strongly

Just as the TOPIC Strategy gives students a mnemonic to help them recall the task components of a persuasive essay or position paper, the POWER Strategy (Englert

& Raphael, 1988) will remind them of the steps necessary for *any* effective writing. In addition to the five steps of the POWER Strategy—*planning, organization, writing, editing,* and *revising*—there is another step, a final "R" for *rereading,* that can further improve the quality of students' writing.

The POWER(R) Strategy

PLANNING

One aspect of writing in which learning disabled students demonstrate particular weakness is *planning,* or *prewriting.* Many LD students suffer from impulsivity, jumping right into a task, which, as we know, is the total opposite of being "planful." Therefore, no writing instruction strategy would be complete without drawing students' attention to the planning stage of the writing task. Figure 3 shows some prewriting strategies.

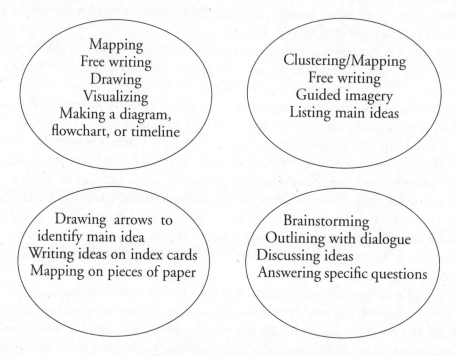

Figure 3: Prewriting Strategies

Planning involves brainstorming, or retrieving background knowledge a student possesses on a particular subject through a process similar to free association. It is an effective way to access information of which the student may be consciously unaware. For example, let us examine a hypothetical essay.

Prompt:
Circumstances often impact personality in such a way that historical contexts define leadership. Conversely, personality and leadership qualities can leave indelible marks on historical eras.

Assignment: Does the leader create history or does history create the leader? Write an essay that expresses your point of view. Include supporting examples and analysis taken from your studies, reading, life experience, or personal observations.

In this assignment, the student should think in terms of a leader and a historical era about which he or she is knowledgeable. To determine whether the student's information is sufficient to fulfill the requirements of the essay, the student must brainstorm background information stored in memory.

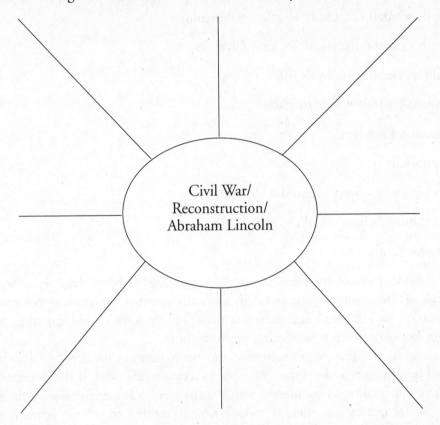

Civil War/
Reconstruction/
Abraham Lincoln

Figure 4: Spider or Web Plan

In the web shown in Figure 4, the student decided to brainstorm the Civil War, Reconstruction, and Abraham Lincoln, on which the student will base his argument, and has placed all three in the center of the web. There are many events and issues associated with the Civil War, so the student can add as many extended lines as needed, writing a particular event related to the Civil War on each line extended from the center. At this stage, the student has not yet formulated a thesis about whether the Civil War impacted Lincoln or whether he impacted the historical event. *Brainstorming background knowledge* is a preliminary and crucial step to creating the thesis.

Some of the facts the student may have recalled during the brainstorming/planning stage are

• Causes—secession, states rights, slavery

• Brother vs. brother

• Bloodiest war

• South fought to preserve way of life

• North fought to preserve the Union

- South had superior military leaders and had "home court advantage"

- North had better transportation, more manufacturing, more money, and more men

- South seceded because of election of Lincoln

- South in economic shambles after Civil War

- Military occupation by North

- How to readmit Southern states?

- Sixteenth President

- Republican

- Lincoln's goal—to preserve the Union

- Gettysburg Address freed slaves in South

- Forgave South

The randomness of the ideas the student generated is perfectly acceptable. The purpose of the brainstorming is (a) to ascertain whether the student has enough information to formulate and defend a thesis on the subject and (b) to generate enough facts to present a convincing position paper.

Once again, this is an opportunity for students to monitor the depth of their background information to determine whether its scope is sufficient. If the student lacks adequate information to complete a web about Lincoln's leadership during the Civil War and Reconstruction, there is enough time to rethink the choice of subject. At this point, the student may decide to brainstorm, for example, the Great Depression, World War II, or the Vietnam War and the impact of that event on presidential leadership. Remember, in providing supporting opinions, students are *not* limited to historical events. The essay instructions state: "Include supporting examples and analysis taken from your studies, reading, life experience, or personal observations." The students' goal is, first and foremost, to support their opinions giving concrete evidence. The source of the evidence is less important than the extent to which it supports the students' thesis.

If the students read the prompt and are not certain how to proceed, they can construct a table in which they weigh the two aspects of the question. See Figure 5 for an example of how to set up a conflicting idea chart.

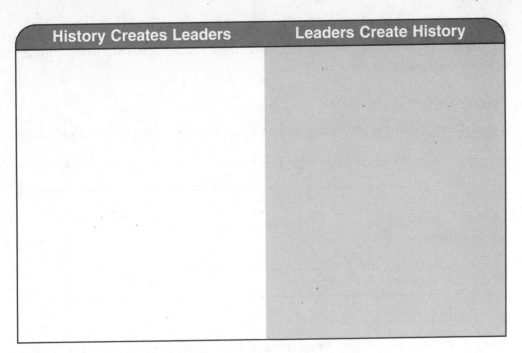

History Creates Leaders	Leaders Create History

Figure 5: Conflicting Idea or Pro/Con Chart

ORGANIZATION

Another stumbling block for LD students is *organization*, the second step in the POWER Strategy. Organization involves

1. Taking the information the student generated during the planning, or brainstorming stage
2. Making decisions about the suitability of the information
3. Eliminating facts that have little or no relevance to the topic
4. Prioritizing the remaining facts based on their importance as persuasive evidence

Thus, in the organization stage, the student returns to the original essay topic and determines the applicability of the information accessed during the planning stage. At this point, the student must determine whether (a) to change topics due to insufficient information, (b) to brainstorm additional facts, or (c) to organize and prioritize the information.

Before writing the persuasive essay or position paper, the student must understand the task, that is, to interpret or form a judgment about the question. The thesis statement will express the student's *opinion*; it is *not* a statement of fact.

Returning to the list of facts on the Civil War/Reconstruction/Abraham Lincoln generated by our hypothetical student, are there sufficient facts to develop a thesis and write a persuasive essay? The student appears to have an adequate fund of background knowledge. However, the student will have to make decisions concerning how to organize and prioritize the facts. The student can employ a variety of methods to organize the information, from basic listing of facts in order of importance to an essay organizer.

To use an essay organizer (see Figure 6), the student must return to the original essay topic to formulate the thesis statement. The thesis statement will guide the essay; therefore, it should be written at the outset, and all statements of fact will be measured according to how well they relate back to the thesis statement. In addition, the student will need to frame approximately three reasons (each ultimately forming a body paragraph) that support the thesis.

Paragraph One—Introduction:

Introductory statement (including historical context and background information):

_____

_____

_____

Thesis statement:

_____

_____

_____

Reasons #1, #2, and #3 to support your thesis statement (from most to least important):

1. _____

_____

_____

2. _____

_____

_____

3. _____

_____

_____

Paragraph Two:

Topic sentence stating Reason#1

_____

_____

_____

Evidence:

1. _____

_____

_____

2. _____

_____

_____

3. _____

_____

_____

Paragraph Three:

Topic sentence stating Reason #2:

_____

_____

_____

Evidence:

1. _____

_____

_____

2. _____

_____

_____

3. _____

_____

_____

Paragraph Four:

Topic sentence stating Reason #3:

_____

_____

_____

Evidence:

1. _____

_____

_____

2. _____

_____

_____

3. _____

_____

_____

Paragraph Five:

Restate thesis statement:

_____

_____

_____

Restate Reasons #3, #2, and #1 (in order from least important to most important):

1. _____

_____

_____

2. _____

_____

_____

3. _____

_____

_____

Figure 6: Essay Organizer

Returning to the original example, the student has decided that the events of the historical era impacted Lincoln's presidential leadership and will state this as a thesis statement. With the thesis statement as a guide, the student will then return to the list of facts to determine a plan of organization. The question will then be: What facts can I use when I formulate reasons to support my thesis statement? While reading the list of facts, the student is making conscious decisions about whether to use a fact or eliminate it, how to use it, or whether to group it with other related facts. For example, "The North fought to preserve the Union" and "Lincoln's goal—to preserve the Union" could be grouped together. Finally, once the student has decided what information can be used to support the thesis, he or she must then prioritize the reasons in order of importance and select the appropriate facts to serve as evidence.

WRITING

Using the information generated during the planning stage, and organizing and prioritizing the information using the essay organizer, the student will have little difficulty writing the essay. For most people, the most difficult aspect of writing is getting started. The blank page is daunting! However, with the essay organizer, the student no longer has to face the writing task unprepared.

A question that is often asked is, "Why is it suggested that I write three reasons in support of the thesis statement and give three pieces of evidence to support the topic sentences? Why 3's?" The answer is simple; the three supporting reasons will eventually generate topic sentences for three body paragraphs. With the introductory paragraph, the concluding paragraph, and the three body paragraphs, the student has a classic five-paragraph essay. However, there is no hard and fast rule that the persuasive essay required on the SAT *must* be a five-paragraph essay. If the student is able to provide convincing evidence to support the thesis in a shorter essay, that is acceptable. The important thing to remember is the task—that is, to support the position the student has taken.

If the student follows the essay organizer, is that sufficient? Without meaning to equivocate, the answer is yes and no. The answer is yes in that the student will have fulfilled the task of writing a convincing persuasive essay; however, the answer is no in that certain conventions of standard written English must be observed, and the vocabulary must be suitable for the level of the audience or the student will not achieve an optimal score. Therefore, the aim is not merely *what* the student says but *how* the student says it. The student should avoid empty words like "important" and "interesting." In addition, students should stay away from slang, colloquialisms, and Instant Message/chat room/e-mail abbreviations. Furthermore, a general rule of thumb is "Never utilize utilize, use use;" meaning that students should, whenever possible, express themselves simply and succinctly, and avoid wordiness.

EDITING

There are two aspects of editing, both of which may present problems for LD students. The first is editing for content; the second is editing for mechanics.

When *editing for content*, the best approach is self-questioning. The student should make a checklist of required elements, perhaps using the TOPIC Strategy as a guide, and use that list to formulate questions. For example:

- Have I opened my essay strongly?

- Do I have a clear thesis statement?

- Do the topic sentences of the body paragraphs relate to my thesis?

- Does the evidence I present in the body paragraphs support the reasons for my thesis?

- Have I proven my thesis?

- Have I concluded my essay with a strong restatement of my thesis and the supporting reasons?

In addition, the student may want to include some general questions that relate to most forms of general written expression:

- Is my writing clear?

- Did I include "empty" words or slang?

- Are my vocabulary and tone suitable for my audience?

- Have I made my writing interesting by varying sentence structure?

- What is the strongest part of my essay?

- What is the weakest part of my essay?

The answers to the self-questioning will enable the student to improve the quality of the essay during the revision stage when using the POWER Strategy.

When *editing for mechanics*, the student should keep several things in mind—punctuation, spelling, usage, agreement, grammar, and the appearance of the essay itself. In addition, while editing the essay, students should look for errors in parallel construction (e.g., He likes hiking, swimming, and to read), in verb tenses (e.g., Yesterday he and his sister shop with their mother); in run-on sentences (e.g., Alan does not enjoy camping instead he prefers playing ball with his friends); and sentence fragments (e.g., Scary ghost stories in the dark). There will be more discussion about grammatical errors later in this chapter. Many LD students are permitted the test modification of "word processor/computer"; however, they should not become dependent on the spell check or grammar check since, during testing, these computer features are frequently disabled. Therefore, the student must rely on his or her own ability to edit.

THE COPS STRATEGY

The *COPS Strategy* (University of Kansas Institute for Research in Learning Disabilities) provides students with a checklist for editing some possible mechanical errors. The acronym COPS, which stands for Capitalization, Overall appearance, Punctuation, and Spelling, enables students to use a self-questioning technique, similar to that used with content editing:

- Have I *capitalized* all proper names (i.e., people, places, documents), as well as the first word of every sentence?

- How would I judge the *overall appearance* of my paper? Are there many erasures? Would the reader look at my paper as being sloppy or unappealing?

- Have I used the proper *punctuation*? Do my sentences end in periods, question marks, or exclamation points? Have I separated items in a series and multiple clauses with commas?

- Have I checked the *spelling* in my essay? Is it correct? Does it conform to the spelling rules I know? Have I avoided the abbreviations of computer communication?

The COPS Strategy

Capitalization

Overall Appearance

Punctuation

Spelling

REVISION

The purpose of editing the essay for both content and mechanics is to enable students to produce the best possible, most error-free pieces of writing that they are capable of producing. Students will vary in their writing abilities, but the purpose of editing and revision is for all students, no matter what their potential, to demonstrate their best writing. To that end, the student must reread his or her essay with a view toward correcting the problems found during self-questioning. If the issue was a lack of clarity, the student must locate the sections of the essay that are unclear. If the essay is wordy, the student must rewrite verbose sentences as simply as possible, eliminating repetitive words and passages as necessary. If the essay is unexciting, perhaps the student should include a "grabber," a sentence or phrase designed to catch the reader's attention. Finally, the student should check the essay for logic (i.e., whether the evidence supports the reasons for the student's beliefs). If the ideas presented in support are a "stretch," the student may wish to revise the essay to either reconstruct or omit weak evidence.

Similarly, mechanical errors should be corrected where possible. Sentences should be revised so that errors in grammar, word usage, subject-verb agreement, spelling, and punctuation are corrected. In addition, any errors that were not caught during editing should be corrected. The revision stage is the student's last chance to impress the reader.

(REREADING)

Normally the POWER Strategy would be complete with the revision stage. However, there is one final step students should take to make certain that they have understood the intent of the task. This can only be done when students *reread* the writing prompt and the assignment. The most complete, well-written essay will still achieve a minimal grade if it does not fulfill the task. Since many LD students have difficulty with reading comprehension, it is essential that students highlight key words and phrases in the writing prompt and assignment during a first reading. In this way, upon rereading the task, students can judge the extent to which their essays have fulfilled the writing assignment.

The POWER(R) Strategy

Planning

Organization

Writing

Editing

Revising

(Rereading)

Application of Strategy

Prompt:
  Benjamin Franklin said: "If you would not be forgotten as soon as you are dead, either write things worth reading or do things worth writing."

Assignment: If you had a choice, would you choose to be one of those who "write things worth reading" or those who "do things worth writing"? Plan and write an essay in which you develop your point of view on this issue. Support your position with reasoning and examples taken from your reading, studies, experience, or observations.

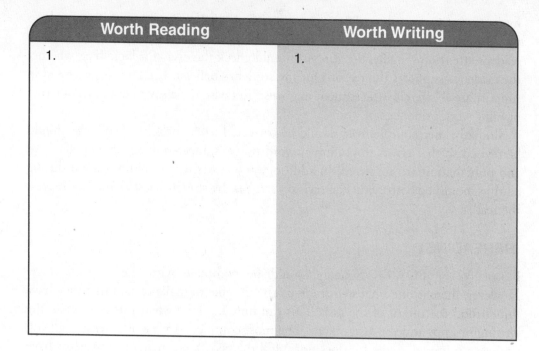

Worth Reading	Worth Writing
1.	1.

Figure 7: Pro/Con Chart

Students should use listing, webs, or pro/con chart like that shown in Figure 7 to brainstorm ideas in support of their opinion. Having completed the organizer, students decide which position to take, and group similar ideas together. Having formed a position, students should decide which arguments are their strongest and then write a thesis statement. Finally, they should frame their ideas using the essay frame format.

Examples of Essay Prompts and Assignments to Be Used with TOPIC and POWER(R) Strategies

Using the following example of essay prompts and assignments, students should practice applying the POWER(R) Strategy, using graphic organizers, pro/con charts, essay frames, lists, or whatever other tools they have developed to help them complete their writing tasks.

1.

Prompt:
   Horace said: "Mistakes are their own instructor."

Assignment: Using contemporary history as a guide, do you agree or disagree with this statement? Plan and write an essay in which you develop your point of view on this issue. Support your position with reasoning and examples taken from your reading, studies, experience, or observations.

2.

> **Prompt:**
>
> Baron de Montesquieu said, "We receive three educations, one from our parents, one from our schoolmaster, and one from the world. The third contradicts all that the first two teach us."
>
> **Assignment:** Does the education we receive from the world in fact contradict what we receive from our parents and teachers? Plan and write an essay in which you develop your point of view on this issue. Support your position with reasoning and examples taken from your reading, studies, experience, or observations.

3.

> **Prompt:**
>
> Robert Heinlein said: "You live and learn or you don't live long."
>
> **Assignment:** Do you believe that education is necessary for survival? Support your position with reasoning and examples taken from your reading, studies, experience, or observations.

4.

> **Prompt:**
>
> Henry Ward Beecher said: "Greatness lies not in being strong, but in the right use of strength."
>
> **Assignment:** Using the history of civilization as a guide, do you agree or disagree with this statement? Plan and write an essay in which you develop your point of view on this issue. Support your position with reasoning and examples taken from your reading, studies, experience, or observations.

GRAMMAR STRATEGIES

In the Improving Sentences, Identifying Sentence Errors, and Improving Paragraphs components, students have a minimum of 35 minutes (a maximum of 70 minutes with double-time testing modification) to answer 49 questions on English grammar and usage. There are few grammar strategies, but there are some tips that may help LD students identify grammatical errors. Unlike the experience of editing one's own essay for mechanical errors where a student is uncertain if a grammatical problem exists, in this section the possible errors are already underlined and choices for improving the error are given. The underlined word or phrase may have no error, so "No error," is one of the choices; however, if an error is present, it will appear in the underlined segment.

Categories of errors appear, so that once a student is familiar with the error categories, this section of the SAT is not quite as daunting as it may appear initially. The purpose of this section is to test students' basic knowledge of Standard English. Often, when asked, students will claim they identified an error because "it sounded wrong." That approach is perfectly sound; it demonstrates a familiarity with correct language. However, there are examples of errors that "sound right" and are still incorrect. For this reason, students can take steps to prepare themselves for the errors commonly found in this section.

The Two-Finger Strategy

A very common error that appears involves *subject-verb agreement.* If asked, most students can identify the subject of a sentence; it is usually the main noun (i.e., person, place, or thing) or pronoun to which or about which the action of the sentence revolves. The verb is the action that is taking place. In a very simple sentence, "Mom cooks," the subject is "Mom" and the verb is "cooks." Sometimes the verb has auxiliary or helping words, for example, "Mom is cooking." In this case, the verb is now two words, "is cooking." Most students know that a singular subject should have a singular verb and a plural subject should have a plural verb. However, it is often confusing in error identification exercises when several words intervene between the subject and the verb. For example, in the sentence, "My cousins, who are the daughters of my favorite aunt, <u>are coming</u> over to visit," there are several words separating the subject, "cousins" and the verb, "are coming." If the sentence read, "My cousins are coming over to visit," there would not be any confusion—plural subject, "cousins," plural verb "are coming." However, because of the intervening phrase, "who are daughters of my favorite aunt," the tendency is to make the verb agree with the noun closest to the verb, "aunt." "Aunt" is singular; therefore, many students, believing there is an error in the underlined verb, would choose "is coming" to correct it. As a result, to minimize the possibility of falling into this trap, students can use the *Two-Finger Strategy.*

First, they should identify the simple subject ("cousins") and the verb ("are coming") and place two fingers, either horizontally or vertically over the intervening words. This effectively blocks out the confusing phrase. Once students have practiced identifying subject-verb agreement prior to the SAT, they will no longer be confused by this type of error.

If students have difficulty locating the subject but are able to locate the verb, using the previous example, they would ask themselves the question, "Who are coming to visit?" and the answer would be "cousins," the subject. Conversely, if students can identify the subject ("cousins") but not the verb, they would ask themselves, "What are the cousins doing?" and the answer, of course, would be that they "are coming."

The Two-Finger Strategy
1. **Read the sentence.**
2. **Identify the subject (main noun or pronoun in the sentence).**
3. **Identify the verb (the action involving the subject).**
4. **Cover the words in between the subject and the verb with two fingers, either horizontally or vertically.**
5. **Check to see if the subject-verb agreement is correct.**

The Two-Finger Strategy can prove very useful to students in another situation. There is another agreement error that often appears in the error identification questions on the SAT—the pronoun–verb agreement. Pronouns take the place of nouns and, as such, they also differ in number. For example, the pronouns "he" and "she" require a singular form of the verb, whereas the pronoun "they" requires a plural form of the verb. That is fairly clear to students; however, the pronouns "everyone," "everybody," "someone," "somebody," "nobody," "no one," "one," "either," "each," and "neither" all require singular verb forms. However, "several," "all," "both," "few," and "many" require plural verb forms. This is not a particularly difficult error to detect if the pronoun and the verb are in close proximity. For example, in the sentence, "Somebody is looking for me," it is easy to spot the singular pronoun–singular verb agreement. However, as with the subject (noun)–verb agreement, when there are several words between the subject (pronoun) and the verb, the agreement becomes more difficult to detect. This is where the Two-Finger Strategy comes in.

Application of Strategy

Note: The vocabulary has been made simpler than what the student may encounter on the SAT for the purpose of learning and applying the strategies.

1. Another example of dangerous snakes <u>are</u> cobras.

   (A) are
   (B) should be
   (C) is
   (D) will be
   (E) is being

2. Waffles and sausages, my favorite breakfast, <u>is being served</u> at the diner.

   (A) is being served
   (B) are being served
   (C) can be served
   (D) would be served
   (E) is not being served

3. The actions of the new mayor <u>hasn't been consistent</u> with his campaign promises.

   (A) hasn't been consistent
   (B) isn't being consistent
   (C) isn't consistent
   (D) haven't been consistent
   (E) has been consistent

4. The city, with its crime rate, dirty streets, and unfriendly strangers, <u>make</u> me long for the quiet countryside.

   (A) make
   (B) has makes
   (C) are making
   (D) have making
   (E) makes

5. Diet and exercise, shown to make people lose weight, <u>have</u> also given me increased energy.

    (A) have
    (B) having
    (C) has
    (D) is having
    (E) has been

Answers and Strategies Applied

1. *Answer:* (C)

   Explanation: In this sentence the student would first identify the subject, "example," and the verb "are." The student would then take two fingers and cover the words "of dangerous snakes." The sentence would read: Another example . . . are cobras (singular subject, plural verb). Therefore, the verb "are" is incorrect in this sentence.

2. *Answer:* (B)

   Explanation: The subject of this sentence is "waffles and sausages" and the verb is "is being served." The student should cover the words between them, "my favorite breakfast" with two fingers. The sentence would then read, "Waffles and sausages . . . is being served." The subject–verb agreement is incorrect (plural subject; singular verb).

3. *Answer:* (D)

   Explanation: In this sentence, the subject is "actions" and the verb is "hasn't." The student would cover "of the new mayor" with two fingers. The resulting sentence is "The actions . . . hasn't been consistent with his campaign promises." The subject–verb agreement is incorrect (plural subject; singular verb).

4. *Answer:* (E)

   Explanation: In this sentence, the subject is "city" and the verb is "make." The student would cover the phrase, "with its crime rate, dirty streets, and unfriendly strangers," with two fingers. The sentence would then read, "The city . . . make me long for the quiet countryside." The subject–verb agreement is incorrect (singular subject; plural verb).

5. *Answer:* (A)

   Explanation: In this sentence, the subject is "diet and exercise" and the verb is "have." The student would cover the phrase, "shown to make people lose weight" with two fingers. The resulting sentence would then read, "Diet and exercise . . . have also given me increased energy." The subject–verb agreement is correct (plural subject; plural verb).

The Box Strategy

Often students will say, "I'm not sure what noun (or pronoun) is the subject." This is particularly true if there are many words intervening between the subject and the verb. For example, in the sentence, "The boy with the red hair in the second row of two of my three classes is my friend," there are 14 words between the subject "boy" and the verb "is." Could "hair" be the subject? Could "row" be the subject? Could "two" be the subject? Could "classes" be the subject? They are all nouns. Those words cannot be the subject of the sentence above because all of them are objects of prepositional phrases. A *prepositional phrase* is, simply put, a phrase that begins with a preposition and ends with a noun or pronoun, the object of the preposition. To eliminate a noun or pronoun as the subject of the sentence, the student must first decide whether it is the object of a prepositional phrase. To do this, the student must be able to identify a preposition. To give a list of prepositions will require that the student memorize them. Instead, students should remember the *Box Strategy* for identifying a preposition—that is, students should picture a box in their minds. Anything in relation to the box is a preposition.

For example, you can sit *in* the box, *inside* the box, *on* the box, *under* the box, *underneath* the box, *over* the box, *along* the box, *with* the box, *within* the box, *by* the box, *above* the box, *beyond* the box, *upon* the box, *near* the box, *behind* the box, *beside(s)* the box, *below* the box; you can go *into* the box or *onto* the box, be *at* the box; walk *through* the box, *to* the box, *toward* the box, *from* the box, *around* the box, and *past* the box. There are a few more prepositions—of, but, among, after—that are admittedly difficult to attach to the box; however, recalling the Box Strategy should help students identify prepositions and, more importantly, prepositional phrases that are placed between subjects and verbs, thus presenting an obstacle to correct agreement.

Application of Strategy

1. Every girl in my classes <u>are going</u> on the trip.

   (A) are going
   (B) is going
   (C) are
   (D) have been
   (E) have gone

2. Three sentences in the paragraph <u>contains</u> inaccuracies.

   (A) contains
   (B) is containing
   (C) are containing
   (D) contain
   (E) will be containing

3. The land under the bridges <u>is</u> swampy.

   (A) is
   (B) is being
   (C) will be
   (D) are
   (E) are becoming

4. The sea to the west and beyond the barrier islands <u>are</u> calm.

    (A) are
    (B) are being
    (C) have been
    (D) is being
    (E) is

5. Each of the Malone sisters <u>are</u> able to sing, dance, and act.

    (A) are
    (B) can
    (C) is
    (D) has been
    (E) have been

Answers and Strategies Applied

1. *Answer:* (B)

   Explanation: The subject–verb agreement is incorrect because "every" is a singular pronoun and "are" is a plural verb. "In my classes" is a prepositional phrase since it begins with the preposition, "in" (in the box).

2. *Answer:* (D)

   Explanation: The subject–verb agreement is incorrect because "sentences" is the subject and therefore the verb must be plural. "In the paragraph" is a prepositional phrase, and the singular noun "paragraph" is an object of the preposition.

3. *Answer:* (A)

   Explanation: The singular subject "land" agrees with the singular verb "is." The plural noun "bridges" is the object of the preposition "under" (the box), not the subject of the sentence.

4. *Answer:* (E)

   Explanation: The subject–verb agreement is incorrect since the subject "sea" is singular and the verb "are" is plural. The noun "west" is the object of the preposition "to" (the box), and the noun "islands" is the object of the preposition "beyond" (the box).

5. *Answer:* (C)

   Explanation: The subject–verb agreement is incorrect since the pronoun "each" is a singular subject and "are" is a plural verb. The noun "sisters" is the object of the preposition "of."

The PACK Strategy

Another common error that is found in the Improving Sentences, Identifying Sentence Errors, and Improving Paragraphs components of the Writing Section of the SAT is the *dangling or misplaced modifier*. Put simply, a word or phrase fails to modify or describe the word intended because of its faulty positioning in a sentence. As a result, it modifies or describes another word in the sentence, or worse, it does not describe or modify any word. For example, in the sentence, "Running across the street, <u>the bus</u> slowed so it would not hit the pedestrian." According to this sentence, the bus was running across the street. Correctly stated it should read: "The bus slowed so it would not hit the pedestrian who was running across the street." The description, in this example, "running across the street," must be located near the word or phrase being modified or described, "the pedestrian." This error is called a *misplaced modifier*.

There are times when a modifier does not modify or describe any word in the sentence. As a result, the sentence is confusing. For example, in the sentence, "Walking on the beach, sand got into our shoes," is the sand walking? If not, who or what is "walking?" Correctly stated, the sentence should read, "Walking on the beach, the girl got sand in her shoes" or "While the girl was walking on the beach, she got sand in her shoes." This error is called a *dangling modifier*.

The *PACK Strategy* can help students identify the modifier and the word that is being modified to determine if the positioning in the sentence is correct. In the first step, students put a circle around the modifying or describing word or phrase. Next, they ask themselves what word or words are being modified or described, if any. Then, they connect the two with a linking motion of their pen or pencil. Finally, students keep the modifier and the words being modified together as they look for a choice among those given in which the positioning of the two is correct. Once students have practiced identifying misplaced and dangling modifiers prior to the SAT, they will no longer be confused by this type of error.

The PACK Strategy

1. **P**ut a circle around the modifying word or phrase.
2. **A**sk what word or words are being modified.
3. **C**onnect the two.
4. **K**eep the modifier and the words modified together when looking for an answer.

Application of Strategy

1. A billionaire bought an island in the South Seas <u>along with his wife</u>.

   (A) A billionaire bought an island in the South Seas along with his wife.
   (B) In the South Seas, a billionaire bought an island along with his wife.
   (C) A billionaire's wife bought an island in the South Seas.
   (D) A billionaire along with his wife bought an island in the South Seas.
   (E) An island along the South Seas was bought by a billionaire's wife.

2. Alone in the house late at night, the howling wind frightened the <u>babysitter</u>.

   (A) Alone in the house late at night, the howling wind frightened the babysitter.
   (B) Alone in the house late at night, the babysitter frightened the howling wind.
   (C) Alone in the house late at night, the babysitter was frightened by the howling wind.
   (D) The howling wind, alone in the house late at night, frightened the babysitter.
   (E) The howling wind frightened the babysitter alone in the house at night.

3. Planning to study, <u>my books and papers</u> were scattered all over the room.

   (A) Planning to study, my books and papers were scattered all over the room.
   (B) Planning to study, I scattered my books and papers all over the room.
   (C) While my books and papers were prepared for study, they were scattered all over the room.
   (D) The room was prepared for studying with books and papers scattered all around.
   (E) My books and papers were scattered all over the room planning to study.

4. While skating on the thin ice, <u>the girl</u> fell into the lake.

   (A) While skating on the thin ice, the girl fell into the lake.
   (B) While skating on the thin ice, into the lake the girl fell.
   (C) The girl, in the lake, fell onto the thin ice.
   (D) The girl on the thin ice on the lake fell in.
   (E) Into the lake, fell the girl on the thin ice.

5. While fixing the roof, <u>the ladder</u> fell.

   (A) While fixing the roof, the ladder fell.
   (B) The ladder fell while fixing the roof.
   (C) As the roof was being fixed, the ladder fell.
   (D) While I was fixing the roof, the ladder fell.
   (E) The ladder fell during the roof being fixed.

Answers and Strategies Applied

1. *Answer:* (D)
   Explanation: The sentence is incorrect because of the faulty positioning of the modifier. The phrase "along with his wife" should modify "the billionaire." The student would put a circle around "along with his wife," ask the word being modified, in this example, "the billionaire," and connect the two with a stroke of a pen. Keeping the modifier and the word being modified together, the student would look among the choices.

2. *Answer:* (C)
   Explanation: The faulty location of the modified word, "babysitter," makes the sentence incorrect. The student should put a circle around the modifier, "Alone in the house at night," and ask who or what is alone in the house late at night. Finding the answer, "the babysitter," the student would connect the two and scan the choices, keeping the relationship between the modifier and the word being modified in mind.

3. *Answer:* (B)
   Explanation: The sentence is incorrect because, as the sentence is written, there is no word being modified. Putting a circle around the modifier, "Planning to study," the student would next ask, "Who is planning to study?" and would then identify that the sentence does not contain a word or words being modified to connect to the modifier. The student must then keep in mind the relationship between the modifier and word being modified when choosing an answer among the choices.

4. *Answer:* (A)

   Explanation: The sentence is correct. The student puts a circle around the modifier, "While skating on the thin ice," and asks "Who is skating on the thin ice?" The student connects "the girl" to the modifier and sees that the sentence keeps them together.

5. *Answer:* (D)

   Explanation: The sentence is incorrect. The student would first put a circle around the modifier, "while fixing the roof." Next, the student would ask, "Who is fixing the roof?" In attempting to identify what is being modified and make a connection, the student would note that there is nothing being modified. At this point, the student would look for a choice that keeps the relationship between the modifier and words modified.

The S-S-D Strategy

Another common error on this section of the SAT is the lack of parallel construction. Simply put, when a sentence has *parallel construction*, it has a similar grammatical pattern. When a sentence lacks parallel construction, it "sounds wrong" and appears to lose rhythm. For example, the sentence, "John likes swimming, jogging, and to play ball," lacks parallel construction because the first and second activities in the series, "swimming" and "jogging," end in *-ing*, and the third activity has "to" before the verb. This is a relatively easy error to spot because it will generally occur only when the sentence contains a series, or list, of items or actions. An easy way for a student to spot errors in parallelism is the *S-S-D Strategy*. As the student notes that the possible error in a sentence or paragraph is within a series, the student should read the series and state which parts of it are constructed the same and which, if any, are constructed differently. For example, the student would read the sentence, "The school was hiring teachers, custodians, and people who cook." Upon a second reading, the student would read, "The school was hiring teachers (*same*), custodians (*same*), and people who cook (*different*)." As sentences become more complicated, identifying errors in parallel construction becomes increasingly more difficult. That is why, a simple strategy like S-S-D, can help students identify similarities and differences.

The student should be aware that a lack of parallelism can exist with only two items. For example, in the sentence, "The couple enjoyed togetherness and <u>to be in harmony</u>," the student would correct "to be in harmony" to "harmony."

The S-S-D Strategy
S – Same
S – Same
D – Different

Application of Strategy

1. The workers wanted higher wages, more sick days, and <u>to have longer vacations</u>.

   (A) The workers wanted higher wages, more sick days, and to have longer vacations.
   (B) The workers wanted higher wages, more sick days, and having longer vacations.
   (C) The workers wanted higher wages, more sick days, and longer vacations.
   (D) The workers wanted to have higher wages, more sick days, and to have longer vacations.
   (E) The workers wanted having higher wages, more sick days, and to have longer vacations.

2. Come to the Islands of Hawaii <u>where you can bask in the sun all day, enjoy the most beautiful scenery in the world, and go surfing in calmest waters</u> on the planet.

   (A) where you can bask in the sun all day, enjoy the most beautiful scenery in the world, and go surfing in calmest waters
   (B) where you can be basking in the sun all day, enjoy the most beautiful scenery in the world, and go surfing in the calmest waters
   (C) where you can bask in the sun all day, be enjoying the most beautiful scenery in the world, and go surfing in calmest waters
   (D) where you can bask in the sun all day, enjoy the most beautiful scenery in the world, and surf in calmest waters
   (E) where you can bask in the sun all day while enjoying the most beautiful scenery in the world and surf in the calmest waters

3. To be successful, a sculptor <u>needs a good studio, adequate light shining in, and having a source of income.</u>

   (A) needs a good studio, adequate light shining in, and having a source of income
   (B) needs having a good studio, adequate light shining in, and having a good source of income
   (C) needs to have a good studio, having adequate light shining in, and having a source of income
   (D) needs a good studio, having adequate light shining in, and a good source of income.
   (E) needs a good studio, adequate light shining in, and a source of income

4. The Preamble of the United States Constitution states: "We the People of the United States, in Order to form a more perfect Union, <u>establish Justice, insure domestic Tranquility, provide for the common defense,</u> promote the general Welfare, and secure the Blessings of Liberty to ourselves and our Posterity, do ordain and establish this Constitution for the United States of America."

   (A) establish Justice, insure domestic Tranquility, provide for the common defense
   (B) establishing Justice, insure domestic Tranquility, and providing for the common defense
   (C) establish Justice, insuring domestic Tranquility, and providing for the common defense
   (D) establish Justice, insure domestic Tranquility, and providing for the common defense
   (E) establish Justice, insuring domestic Tranquility, and provide for the common defense

5. Society should provide citizens with the opportunity <u>to work for their present needs and saving for their future needs.</u>

   (A) to work for their present needs and saving for their future needs
   (B) to work for their present needs and to save for their future needs
   (C) for working for their present needs and to save for their future needs.
   (D) to work at saving for their present needs and also to save for the future
   (E) working for their present needs and also to save for their future needs

Answers and Strategies Applied

1. *Answer:* (C)
   Explanation: Reading the sentence the second time, the student would look at the construction of the series: "higher wages (*same*), more sick days (*same*), and to have longer vacations (*different*)." The sentence lacks parallel construction.

2. *Answer:* (D)
   Explanation: In a sentence such as the above example in which each member of the series contains many words, the student must identify the main word in the series. In the above sentence, the main word in each item is a verb—bask (*same*), enjoy (*same*), and go surfing (*different*).

3. *Answer:* (E)
   Explanation: The above sentence has a series of nouns, two of which are parallel in construction:, studio (*same*) and light (*same*). Adding the word, "having," to "source of income" creates an error in parallelism.

4. *Answer:* (A)
   Explanation: Isolating the part of speech of all the key words in the series—"form," "establish," "insure," "provide," "promote," and "secure"—the student is able to note that there is, in fact, parallel construction.

5. *Answer:* (B)

Explanation: Although there are only two ideas in the above sentence, there is an error in parallel construction. The first "opportunity" is "to work" and the second is "saving," demonstrating a lack of parallelism. When there are only two items, the student must choose an answer that makes the construction of the second the *same* as the first.

The Huh? Strategy

Although there are many possible sentence errors, two that are relatively common are the sentence fragment and the run-on sentence. In the sentence fragment, too little information is given, and in the run-on sentence, too much information is given.

A complete sentence consists of the subject and the verb. Although only two words, the sentence, "Birds fly," is complete. A *sentence fragment* occurs when either the subject or the verb is missing, leading the reader to say, "Huh?" As a result, the best strategy for identifying a sentence fragment is the *Huh? Strategy*; when students find themselves asking "Huh?" they know something is missing. For example, "The best prices anywhere." Huh? Where can one find the best prices anywhere? What are the best prices anywhere? Something is missing. "Spends too much money?" "Huh?" Who spends too much money? Again, something is missing. However, do not confuse a sentence fragment with a command in which the subject is understood. For example, somebody might shout, "Run!" in the case of a fire. The subject is "you," but in an imperative situation, the verb "run" alone can stand as a complete sentence. This "you understood" exception is uncommon and is present only in the case of a command. It is rare that the student would encounter a sentence of this type on the SAT.

The reaction of the reader is similar when the opposite, a run-on sentence, occurs but for a different reason: The reader gets lost because so much information is given. The *run-on sentence* is basically two or more sentences that are strung together without benefit of punctuation. In the example, "John went to play ball he had ice cream he went home," again the reader says, "Huh?" There are three separate sentences— "John went to play ball," "he had ice cream," and "he went home"—strung together. Sometimes run-on sentences can be corrected by the addition of punctuation, and sometimes students should add transition words. For example, the above run-on sentence could be corrected by adding commas and creating a series: "John played ball, had ice cream, and went home." This does not change the meaning of the sentence, but it does add clarity. Run-on sentences typically appear in the Improving Sentences component of the SAT; the student is more likely to encounter short, choppy sentences, in the Improving Paragraphs component. The short, choppy sentences in the example above—"John played ball. He had ice cream. He went home."—are *not* run-on sentences, but they do require improvement. Usually when a sentence of this sort is underlined, it indicates that the student should combine the sentences much as was done above.

Application of Strategy

1. By planning the airport in a rural area instead of the middle of the city, the Planning Commission <u>is avoiding excessive traffic this is a major annoyance to the townspeople</u>.

    (A) is avoiding excessive traffic this is a major annoyance to the townspeople
    (B) will avoid excessive traffic this is a major annoyance to the townspeople
    (C) is avoiding excessive traffic, which is a major annoyance to the townspeople
    (D) is avoiding excessive traffic this can be a major annoyance to the townspeople
    (E) will avoid the major annoyance to the townspeople by excessive traffic

2. <u>Slipping on the ice and falling in a snow drift</u>.

    (A) Slipping on the ice and falling in a snow drift.
    (B) Slipping on the ice a snow drift was falling
    (C) Slipping on the ice and falling in a snow drift every day.
    (D) Slipping on the ice and falling in a snow drift can be dangerous.
    (E) Both slipping on the ice and falling in a snow drift.

3. <u>Take your umbrella it might rain</u>.

    (A) Take your umbrella it might rain.
    (B) Take your umbrella because it might rain.
    (C) Taking your umbrella making it rain.
    (D) Take your umbrella. It might rain.
    (E) Taking your umbrella it might rain.

4. The truth about all things will come out in the end of the <u>book when the hero tells the truth about the characters and what made them do </u>what they did to the members of their families, and what they did to all the other characters too.

    (A) book when the hero tells the truth about the characters and what made them do
    (B) book when the hero tells the truth. About the characters and what made them do
    (C) book and when the hero tells the truth about the characters and what made them do
    (D) book when the hero tells the truth about the characters. And what made them do
    (E) book when the hero tells the truth about the characters, what made them do

5. <u>A hurricane with high winds and torrential rains is threatening the coast</u>.

    (A) A hurricane with high winds and torrential rains is threatening the coast.
    (B) A hurricane on the coast is threatening with high winds and torrential rains.
    (C) A hurricane is threatening the coast with high winds and torrential rains.
    (D) High winds and torrential rains with a hurricane are threatening the coast.
    (E) The coast is being threatened by a hurricane with high winds and torrential rains.

Answers and Strategies Applied

1. *Answer:* (C)

   Explanation: This is clearly a run-on sentence. It could be divided into two short, choppy sentences. However, a better solution is using the word "which" to connect the two sentences.

2. *Answer:* (D)

   Explanation: As written, this is a sentence fragment lacking a verb. Adding the verb "can be" transforms the fragment into a sentence.

3. *Answer:* (B)

   Explanation: As with Question 1, this is a run-on sentence as written. It could be divided into two short, choppy sentences; however, inserting "because" makes the sentence more effective because it creates a causal relationship between the umbrella and the rain.

4. *Answer:* (E)

   Explanation: This sentence as written is a run-on sentence. It can be corrected by creating a series with the appropriate commas as in sentence e, or by dividing the sentence into smaller sentences. However, that was not provided as an option.

5. *Answer:* (A)

   Explanation: The sentence fulfills the requirements of a complete sentence. It contains a subject and a verb, and the modifier of the subject, hurricane, "with high winds and torrential rains" is located correctly in the sentence.

There are other possible types of errors in the Improving Sentences, Identifying Sentence Errors, and Improving Paragraphs components of the SAT. However, if students familiarize themselves with the various types of errors and, particularly, with how to correct these errors, they should not have difficulty with this section. As a reminder, students should practice all strategies before the test date and should use them only when they feel they have taken ownership of the strategies and are comfortable enough applying them.

The Math Section

CHAPTER 4

It's really hard for me to understand how I can do so well in school in math and then bomb on the math part of the SAT. I learned it all—algebra, geometry, word problems—and I ace my tests in school. I even do peer tutoring. My teacher said that maybe I get nervous on the test and mess up the calculation or I feel rushed. That can't be the problem because I use a calculator and I have extended time on the test. Something else is wrong! I need a good score in math because that's my strongest area. I was always a good math student and I was hoping to get into a technical college or engineering school. I can't understand it.

Marisa, 18-year-old senior

HOW LEARNING DISABILITIES AFFECT STUDENT PERFORMANCE IN THE MATH SECTION OF THE SAT

How many students experience the same confusion and frustration as Marisa? They have always received high math grades in school, and have no problem with computation or in conceptualizing math. Why then do they repeatedly do poorly in this section? This chapter will offer some possible explanations as well as strategies to help students like Marisa perform to their best abilities.

In theory, the Math Section of the SAT should be the section of the exam on which learning-disabled students do well because the math concepts from which the SAT draws are ones with which they are familiar. There are few surprises on the Math Section because it is the section of the test most directly based on the school math curriculum (i.e., numerical operations, algebra, geometry, statistics, etc.). In addition, students are permitted to use calculators to assist them with computation, and, at least in the multiple-choice section, students are able to eliminate obviously incorrect answers since such answers will not appear among the choices. Why then do many LD students like Marisa above do poorly on the Math Section? What are the factors that apparently interfere with student success?

The following are just some of the problems many LD students, and, to some extent, all students face on the Math Section of the SAT:

• Too much reliance on the calculator

• Lack of familiarity with the language of math

• Confusion about information required by question

- Poor use of time

- Answering too many/few questions

- Impulsivity, that is, not examining all the choices

- Inability to locate clues within the test

- Test anxiety

As with the Critical Reading Section, students can ease much of their pretest anxiety by becoming familiar with the test format and test directions as part of their advance preparation. The truth remains that, unlike the Critical Reading Section, which has no direct parallel in the student's school experience, the Math Section of the SAT is *just* a cumulative math test where the goal is simply to arrive at solutions to straightforward math problems. As with any math test, *studying and preparation are essential* to student success. However, *unlike* a classroom math test, the *application of test-taking strategies* is just about as important as actual knowledge of math.

Even though students with reading problems may do well on math computation, they are at a disadvantage on an exam such as the SAT where many of the problems involve reading and interpretation. There is much evidence that points to the fact that reading impacts student performance on word problems and math reasoning. Therefore, those students with poor reading comprehension frequently do not perform optimally in the Math Section.

How can students maximize their success? Unlike the Critical Reading Section where students often encounter unfamiliar vocabulary, most students are acquainted with the math vocabulary, having been exposed to it since elementary school. (See Appendix B for math vocabulary.)

Since the Math section provides formulas and facts, memorization is not necessary. However, students must develop familiarity with the application of the formulas through repeated practice. Because there are few surprises in this section, students who have coached themselves in the *language of math*, acquainted themselves with *test directions*, and reviewed *math concepts* should feel relatively comfortable with the Math Section.

General Preparation Strategies for the Math Section

1. **Study** the math terminology provided in Appendix B.
2. **Review** concepts in algebra and geometry as well as basic number facts.
3. **Familiarize** yourself with test directions.
4. **Practice** applying the formulas and facts provided in the Math Section.
5. **Take** several examinations to acquaint yourself with test format.

The purpose of Chapter 4 is *not* to teach math curriculum; that has been done in school and in the abundant math review books on the market. The intention of this chapter is to maximize student success by providing students with *test-specific strategies.*

CALCULATOR STRATEGY

Educators have been debating the benefits of calculators to students since their widespread use. The most common argument against their use is that calculators make students "lazy," that is, they reduce the need for students to do their own computation. The example that is most commonly given on this side of the debate is how supermarket and department store check-out personnel are unable to compute sales totals when scanners break down. In other words, calculator detractors say technology is causing math computation skills to diminish.

The other side of the argument is that students benefit in both speed and accuracy from calculator use. The latter position certainly carries much weight, especially with many LD students for whom accuracy in basic computation may be a problem. Why then haven't the SAT scores in math improved significantly since LD students have been permitted to use calculators?

Before discussing issues of calculator use, some general cautions should be noted:

1. Students should *not* use a calculator for the first time the day of the exam; they should be familiar with all functions prior to the SAT.
2. Students should be familiar with the types of calculators permitted on the exam.
3. If the calculator being used on the exam is one that the student regularly uses, the batteries should be checked prior to the day of the SAT.

As a general rule, the calculator should alleviate students' test anxiety, not contribute to it. Therefore, keeping the above factors in mind, we can now proceed to the actual use of the calculator on the exam and what pitfalls to avoid.

Earlier, it was stated that one of the problems many LD students, and students in general, face on the Math Section of the SAT is an over-reliance on calculators, or rather a blind acceptance of calculator output. Calculators do *not* have thinking mechanisms; the information output by a calculator is only as accurate as the information input. Frequently students input incorrect numbers due to transposition, or reversal, of numbers. Occasionally, under conditions of test anxiety, students forget which number is entered in the calculator first and which number second. For example, in problems of discount percentages, a question may read, "A discount of 20 percent was applied to the original price of $120.00. How much was the discount?" or "How much was the sale price?" Assuming the calculator does not have a percentage function key, the student must remember to enter $120.00 prior to multiplying by 0.20. Students must *think the question through* and ask themselves exactly what it is they are trying to find out. Although the difficulty is seemingly simple, responding to what the question is asking is *the* major problem students face on the Math Section of the SAT, and it will be discussed at length later in this chapter.

Another thing for students to remember is that they must *write the equation or problem* on their scrap paper *before* they attempt any calculation. In this way, they have a direction to follow in order to answer the question. If there is an error in their calculation, they can return to the equation or problem and begin again from that point.

The C-E-O Strategy

How can students avoid some of the main problems inherent in calculator use? There are several factors a student needs to keep in mind to guarantee that the input is correct. By following the *C-E-O Strategy* of calculator use, students should remember to check input, estimate, and deal with one number at a time.

CHECK INPUT

Take the time to check each number that will be entered in the calculator. For students with transposition, or reversal, issues, each number should be covered horizontally with a finger when being entered in the calculator. For example, some students reading the number 346 may transpose the number to 643. It is easy to see how this would result in an incorrect answer. In this situation, the student should cover the 4 and 6, leaving only the 3 exposed, and then enter the 3 in the calculator. Moving further to the right, the student should then cover the 6, leaving the 4 exposed, and enter that into the calculator. Finally, the student should uncover the 6 and enter that number. Similarly, in adding or subtracting individual columns of numbers, the student may want to cover each number vertically as it is entered in the calculator. If the student feels more comfortable using the answer sheet, a tissue, or any other substitute to cover individual numbers, that is perfectly acceptable and is still a good method to isolate numbers and prevent transposition or reversal. Although this process may appear to be time-consuming, it helps to ensure accurate input and, therefore, accurate output.

ESTIMATE, ESTIMATE, ESTIMATE

In the lower grades, students are taught to estimate their answers by rounding out, first single numbers, then additional columns of numbers, to the nearest digit by increasing a number to the next higher number if the number in the column on the right is equal to or greater than 5. For example, if the number 47 is to be rounded to the nearest ten, the estimated number would be 50, since 7 is higher than 5. Similarly, if the number 4,572,328 is to be rounded to the nearest million, the answer would be 5,000,000, since the number to the right of the 4 in the millions column is equal to or greater than 5.

Most elementary school children become fairly competent at estimation, and yet, few carry this very necessary skill into the higher grades. For students using calculators, quick estimations enable them to check whether they might have made an error inputting the numbers. For example, if a student is subtracting 983 from 1,634, students should round the 983 to 1,000 and the 1,634 to 1,600. The estimated answer is 600; the actual answer is 651. This gives the student a gauge by which to determine whether an answer makes sense and is, therefore, a student's quick check of input accuracy. If, however, the student arrived at a difference of 1,000, or, if the student had entered the 983 first and attempted to subtract the 1,634 from 983 thus arriving at a negative number, the student would know immediately that an error had been made. In this situation, it is worth taking the time to estimate in order to give the student a means of checking the eventual answer. Finally, having established an estimate, the student is then ready to calculate and compare the answer to the estimate.

ONE NUMBER AT A TIME

Once the student has reached an answer, care should be given to record the numbers one at a time on the answer sheet from left to right. If necessary, the student can again cover the numbers with a piece of paper or a finger, revealing numbers from left to right. By entering one number at a time, students who reverse numbers can be certain that they are actually recording the numbers correctly. Finally, students must recheck their answers.

The C-E-O Strategy

Check input

Estimate, estimate, estimate

One number at a time

Application of Strategy

1. Estimate 6,432 to the nearest ten.

2. Estimate 6,235,764 to the nearest thousand.

3. Estimate 172,689,531 to the nearest hundred million.

4. Estimate 6.238 to the nearest hundredth.

5. Estimate 4.3995 to the nearest whole number.

Answers and Strategies Applied

1. *Answer:* 6,430
    Explanation: To estimate, it is necessary to look to the right of the number place that is being estimated. The question calls for an estimation to the nearest ten. Therefore, it is necessary to look at the number in the ones place to see if it is more or less than 5. Since 2 is less than 5, the number in the tens column does not increase.

2. *Answer:* 6,236,000
    Explanation: To estimate to the nearest thousand, it is necessary to look at the number in the hundreds column to the right. The number is greater than 5, so the number in the thousands column increases to 6.

3. *Answer:* 200,000,000
    Explanation: To estimate to the nearest hundred million, it is necessary to locate the number in the hundred million column and look at the number to its immediate right to see whether it is more or less than 5. Since the number is 7, the number in the hundred million column increases from 1 to 2.

4. *Answer:* 6.24
    Explanation: To estimate to the nearest hundredth, it is necessary to first examine the numbers to the right of the decimal sign and then locate the number to the right of the hundredth place in the thousandth column to determine if it is

more or less than 5. Because it is greater than 5, the number in the hundredth column increases to 4.

5. *Answer:* 4

   Explanation: Since the number to the immediate right of the whole number in the tenths place is less than 5, the whole number remains 4.

GEOMETRY STRATEGIES

Many students with learning disabilities have the least difficulty with the geometry questions in the Math Section of the SAT for several reasons.

- Reference information is provided that includes the formulas for the area and circumference of a circle, the area of a rectangle and a triangle, the volume of a rectangular solid and a cylinder, the Pythagorean theorem, special right triangles, the number of degrees in a circle, and the sum of the measures in degrees of the angles of a triangle. This minimizes the pressure to retrieve these facts from long-term memory.

- In most cases, choices can be eliminated by merely estimating answers rather than completing full calculations.

- Students are *not* required to provide geometric proofs or to recall theorems.

- Because most of the geometry questions contain drawings, there is a minimal need for reading.

Geometry questions comprise about one-third of the Math Section. Although most students with reading or language-processing disabilities generally have the *least* difficulty with geometry questions, geometry can still pose major problems for students with visual-spatial disabilities. For this reason, students should provide proof of this disability as documented by an educational evaluator or a neuropsychologist to the College Board well before the testing date so that, if eligible, they may have an enlarged copy of the SAT provided to them. The enlargement may ameliorate some of the visual perceptual issues.

Eye-Pencil Rule

Assuming again that students have adequately prepared themselves by reviewing geometric facts, the students' best friends in answering these questions are their eyes and their pencils; that is, students must *use their eyes* to quickly approximate relationships such as angles or comparative lengths when representations are given, and must *use their pencils* to draw figures when none are present or to redraw figures that are not drawn to scale. For example, the following is a word problem with no picture provided:

The length of a rectangular rug is 3 feet more than its width. If the length of the rug is 9 feet, what is the area of the rug in square feet?

    (A) 36 feet
    (B) 48 feet
    (C) 54 feet
    (D) 64 feet
    (E) 72 feet

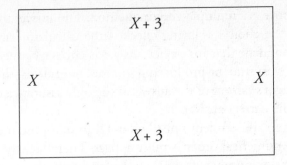

Figure 8: Example of Eye-Pencil Rule

First, students must use their pencils to draw a rectangle and use their eyes to visualize and create approximately the same dimensions stated in the question, which is a rectangle whose length is 3 feet more than the width (see Figure 8). Plugging in the next facts given, the question states that the length is 9 feet. If the length is 3 feet more than the width, the width must be 9 minus 3 or 6 feet. Using the formula for a rectangle ($A = lw$), we multiply 9×6 and find that the answer is 54 or choice (c). This is an example of a geometry question made easier by drawing a representation to scale.

Eye-Pencil Rule

Students should
Use their eyes to quickly approximate relationships and
Use their pencils to draw figures when none are present or figures are not drawn to scale

Geometry Steps Strategy

Sometimes a student will find that a geometry question contains a drawing with the statement, "not drawn to scale." In this situation, it may be worth the student's time to redraw the picture using the correct scale since the incorrect representation may interfere with the student's ability to visualize relationships within the picture.

The first step then in answering a geometry question is *self-questioning*. Students need to ask themselves, "What information is being given and what information is the question asking me to provide?" For this reason, students should underline key words and, when not provided, *draw pictures*.

Next, students should *plug in* the exact numbers provided in the question in order to label the diagram and determine exactly what specific information is given and what is needed. For example, in the above question, the student is told that the length of the rectangle's side is 3 feet longer than the width and that the length is 9 feet. That information enables the student to calculate that the width must be 6 feet. The answer does not end with the width. Returning once more to the question, the student learns that the answer requires the area of the rectangle in feet. The student is then able to plug the numbers into the formula for the area of a rectangle, that is length × width, in order to arrive at 54.

The question above is a multiple-choice question. The answer the student has calculated is among the choices. Having checked the calculator entries, the student should be fairly confident that his or her answer is correct because it is among the choices. However, with student-produced responses, or grid-ins, there are no choices given, and the student's *recheck* of the answer is the only assurance the student has of having arrived at the correct answer.

For grid-in answers, the student must be careful to transpose the answer onto the grid in exactly the numerical order it must appear. Therefore, the earlier calculator strategy for transposing numbers from the calculator onto the paper covering numbers from left to right is the same that the student would use on the grid-ins. The numbers should be transposed into the empty boxes at the top of the grid-ins columns. After the numbers are in the correct column, the student must then go down the column and *locate* the correct number, coloring in the circles corresponding to the number above. Using the correct answer above, 54, the student would cover the 4 with his or her finger, write the 5 at the top of the grid-in, followed by the 4. The student would then return to the column of numbers under the 5 and, using a finger to follow the number vertically, color in the circle next to the 5 completely. Next, the student would do the same with the 4, following the numbers with a finger down the column until arriving at the 4 and then color in the circle completely. A quick scan of the written number, 54, at the top of the grid-in sheet would allow the student to double-check that the numbers circled are correct. Since there is no penalty for guessing among the student-produced responses, students should attempt them *unless* the answer requires much time-consuming calculation that could be better spent on easier questions.

Here's one other caution: On geometry questions, the answers usually depend on fairly concrete facts about geometric relationships that students will have learned in their math courses, as well as the formulas that are provided. If students find that the question requires lengthy calculations, they should go on to the next question and perhaps return to the question later. Students should make some kind of notation next to those questions to which they intend to return if time permits.

Geometry Steps Strategy

- **Self-question** to determine what the question is asking.

- **Draw** a picture representing the figure if not provided; if provided, draw a picture representing the scale.

- **Plug in** the numbers.

- **Do** the calculation.

- **Recheck.**

- **Locate** answer among the choices (or grid-in correct answer).

Application of Strategy

1. The length of a room is 3 feet longer than its width. It will require 102 square feet of carpeting to cover the floor. What is the length and width of the room?

   (A) 12×18
   (B) 18×24
   (C) 24×27
   (D) 27×36
   (E) 36×48

2. The perimeter of an isosceles triangle is 70 cm. The base is 10 cm more than the sides. What is the measurement of the base?

   (A) 15
   (B) 20
   (C) 30
   (D) 40
   (E) 60

3. A piece of wrapping paper measuring $4x + 2$ long by $10x$ wide is folded widthwise. The perimeter of the new piece of paper is 58. What is the length and width?

   (A) 14×15
   (B) 16×18
   (C) 15×18
   (D) 18×24
   (E) 20×25

4. Find the perimeter of a rectangle whose sides measure $9x + 10$ and $5x + 2$.

   (A) $4x + 8$
   (B) $9x + 12$
   (C) $12x + 20$
   (D) $20x + 22$
   (E) $28x + 24$

5. A rectangle has a perimeter of 64 cm. The length is 2 cm greater than the width. Find the length and width of the rectangle.

   (A) 9×12
   (B) 15×17
   (C) 16×28
   (D) 20×24
   (E) 22×24

Answers and Strategies Explained

1. *Answer:* (C)

   Explanation: According to the Geometry Steps Strategy, the first step is to self-question what the question is asking. This is asking for the length and width of the rectangle. Next, the student must draw a figure in which the length is 3 feet longer than the width.

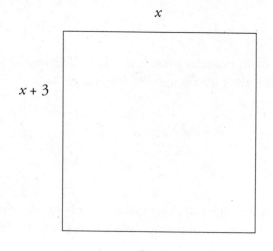

Figure 9

Next, the student needs to plug in the numbers:

$$x + x + x + 3 + x + 3 = 102$$

The next step would be to do the calculation:

$$4x + 6 = 102$$
$$4x + 6 - 6 = 102 - 6$$
$$\frac{4x}{4} = \frac{96}{4}$$
$$x = 24$$

To recheck, insert the numbers into the equation in place of the variable, x:

$$24 + 24 + 24 + 3 + 24 + 3 = 102$$

Finally, the student should go back to the original problem and answer the question:

$$\text{width } (x) = 24$$
$$\text{length } (x + 3) = 27$$

2. *Answer:* (C)

   Explanation: In the first step, the student self-questions what the question is asking and finds that it wants the student to determine the length of the triangle's base. Next, the student must draw a picture representing the isosceles triangle with each side represented by the variable x and the base by x + 10:

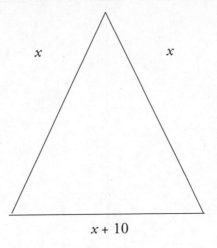

$$x + 10$$

Figure 10

The student then plugs in the numbers:

$$x + x + x + 10 = 70$$

Next, the student does the calculation:

$$3x + 10 = 70$$
$$3x + 10 - 10 = 70 - 10$$
$$\frac{3x}{3} = \frac{60}{3}$$
$$x = 20$$

The student then rechecks the calculation by inserting the numbers back into the equation:

$$20 + 20 + 20 + 10 = 70$$

Finally, the student answers the question.

$$\text{Base} = x\,(20) + 10 = 30$$

3. *Answer:* (A)

Explanation: First, the student self-questions to determine what is being asked. The question calls for the student to find the length of the sides of the folded piece of paper. The student must draw a representation of the figure:

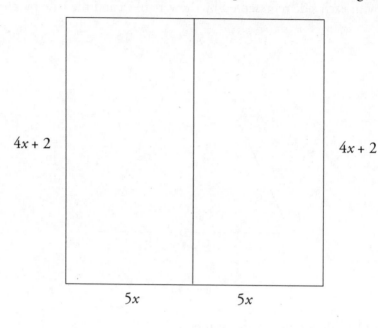

Figure 11

Next, the student must plug in the numbers:

$$4x + 2 + 4x + 2 + 5x + 5x = 58$$

The student then does the calculation:

$$18x + 4 = 58$$
$$18x + 4 - 4 = 58 - 4$$
$$\frac{18x}{18} = \frac{54}{18}$$
$$x = 3$$

Next, the student must recheck the calculation by inserting the numbers into the original equation in place of the variables.

$$4(3) + 2 + 4(3) + 2 + 5(3) + 5(3) = 58$$

Finally, the student is able to answer the question:

Length = 14
Width = 15

4. *Answer:* (E)

   Explanation: In this equation, the student is *not* asked to solve for the variable; rather, the student is asked to express the perimeter of the rectangle by simplifying the terms of the equation. In the second step of the strategy, the student draws the rectangle.

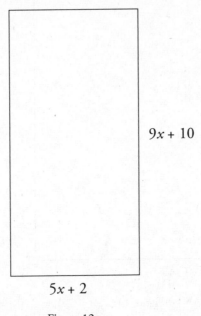

$9x + 10$

$5x + 2$

Figure 12

Next, the student plugs in the numbers as if to solve the equation:

$$9x + 10 + 9x + 10 + 5x + 2 + 5x + 2$$

The student then simplifies the equation by combining like terms:

$$28x + 24$$

The student can recheck the calculation:

$$2(9x) + 2(5x) = 28x$$
$$2(10) + 2(2) = 24$$

5. *Answer:* (B)

Explanation: The student must first self-question to determine that the information needed is the length and the width and then draw a diagram to approximate the measurements given.

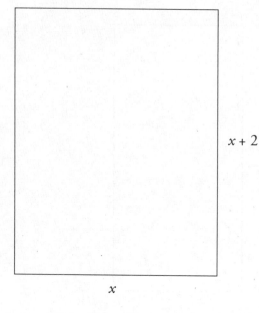

Figure 13

Next, the student needs to plug the numbers and variables into the equation:

$$x + 2 + x + 2 + x + x = 64$$

The student then does the calculation:

$$4x + 4 = 64$$
$$4x + 4 - 4 = 64 - 4$$
$$\frac{4x}{4} = \frac{60}{4}$$
$$x = 15$$

Next, the student rechecks:

$$15 + 2 + 15 + 2 + 15 + 15 = 64$$

Finally, the student looks for the answer to the question:

$$\text{Length} = x\,(15) + 2 = 17$$
$$\text{Width} = x = 15$$

WORD PROBLEM STRATEGIES

Students who have learning disabilities or who learn differently seem to have the greatest problems with word problems. There are several reasons for this.

- *Reading:* Because word problems are equally dependent on reading as math skills, many students who have decoding or reading comprehension difficulties find word problems confusing and time-consuming.

- *Vocabulary:* Because word problems are written using the specialized vocabulary of math, students must

  a. Understand the vocabulary embedded in the problem
  b. Apply specific understanding of math concepts to solve the problem
  c. Answer the question by applying the language of math

In short, the task requires that the student transfer words into symbols and then back to words. For students who have failed to master the specific language of math, interpretation of word problems is extremely difficult.

- *Memory:* The ability to solve word problems also depends on the retention of cumulative math concepts learned over many years. For students with storage, retrieval, and/or long-term memory deficits, these types of questions may pose particular difficulties. Often the recall of specific information, such as the order of operations, decimal/fraction relationships, and manipulation of negative numbers are required.

- *Application:* Remembering math facts is just a small part of word problems; students must then apply the concepts to determine what math operation is necessary. Therefore, these questions depend on student interpretation, judgment, and mastery of mathematical concepts. Thus, solving word problems involves a two-step operation (i.e., interpretation and application).

- *Extrapolation:* Finally, the solving of word problems is a factor of extrapolating unknown information from the information that is given. In this way, interpretation of word problems is a prerequisite for success in algebra.

- *Attention:* In addition to problems with reading, vocabulary, recall, and an inability to extrapolate relevant information, students with attentional issues may find it difficult to maintain the concentration and perseverance necessary to carry out multistep word problems.

Since students' success in algebra depends, to a large extent, on their ability to solve word problems, it is important that students identify and use strategies as tools to assist them on these questions. Most strategies involve what LeBlanc (1977) identifies as four stages in the solution of word problems: (1) understanding the problem, (2) planning the solution, (3) solving the problem, and (4) reviewing the problem.

In translating these stages to the word problems found on the SAT, students should be performing an **eight-step process**. These steps are

1. *Read* the word problem very carefully
2. *Identify* what information is necessary to solve the problem
3. *Select* the mathematical concepts necessary
4. *Apply* the correct concept
5. *Carry out* the necessary mathematical operations
6. *Recheck*
7. *Reread* the problem
8. *Select* the correct answer among the choices

The Self-Questioning Strategy

Students will perform the initial step, reading the word problem, and the final step, selecting the correct answer, automatically. However, students may require a prompt to carry out the middle steps. While practicing word problems, students may find it helpful to carry three index cards as prompts for the *Self-Questioning Strategy*:

The first index card would contain the question, *"What information that is given do I need to solve this problem?"* Upon reading this, the student would identify relevant information in the problem. The second index card would contain the question, *"What mathematical operations should I use to solve this problem?"* This would prompt the student to (a) focus on clues in the language of the problem (e.g., difference, each, together, sum, product) and (b) select the necessary operation. The third index card would contain the question, *"What information that I need to solve this problem is unknown?"* This prompts the student to evaluate the question for information needed that the problem does not supply. In simple questions, the unknown is the answer. In multi-step problems, students may have to perform several operations, adding unknown information, just to arrive at the answer.

Eventually, through the use of the index cards acting as concrete prompts during practice sessions, the students will internalize self-questioning and perform it automatically.

Self-Question Strategy (Using Index Card Prompts)

Card #1: What information that is given do I need to solve the problem?

Card #2: What mathematical operations should I use to solve this problem?

Card #3: What information that I need to solve this problem is unknown?

The CUDGEL Strategy

A basic problem-solving strategy that assists students in recalling the steps to solving a word problem is the *CUDGEL Strategy*. CUDGEL is a mnemonic that stands for *compute* (or simplify) the numbers given in a problem, *use* a formula that applies to the type of problem, *draw* an aid (model, diagram, picture, table, chart, or list), *guess* (or estimate) an answer, *eliminate* unnecessary information, and *logically apply* all clues. This strategy is general enough to be applied to most word problems.

The CUDGEL Basic Problem-Solving Strategy

Compute or simplify numbers

Use a formula that applies

Draw an aid (chart, table, diagram, picture, model)

Guess or estimate an answer

Eliminate any unnecessary information

Logically apply clues

Concrete-to-Representational-to-Abstract Sequence of Problem-Solving

Mercer et al. (1996) identified *Concrete-to-Representational-to-Abstract (C-R-A)* as a sequence by which students with learning disabilities might learn and apply mathematical knowledge to word problems.

At the *concrete* stage, which may occur in school, students are directly instructed in math concepts. In lower grades, this may be done through manipulatives. On the secondary level, teachers and tutors may occasionally use beans or specific objects in the course of direct instruction in math skills.

At the *representational* stage, students move away from the specific, concrete aids used by teachers or tutors in class during direct instruction to creating their own representations or drawings of the information provided in the word problems. As students progress to algebraic word problems, the ability to draw picture representations of problems becomes more important.

At the *abstract* stage, students are no longer dependent on concrete aids or their own diagrams; they are able to use only the mathematical symbols and language of the word problem to arrive at a solution. In algebraic word problems with one variable, students often are able to progress through the C-R-A sequence. However, with multistep problems, it may be advisable for students to continue using diagrams and representations in arriving at solutions. In the next section, the C-R-A Sequence will be applied to algebraic word problems.

Concrete-Representational-Abstract Sequence of Problem-Solving

Concrete Stage: Students use concrete aids to master math concepts (e.g., beans).

Representational Stage: Students draw diagrams representing information.

Abstract Stage: Students use only the information provided in the problem.

ALGEBRA STRATEGIES

Algebra is arguably the most difficult area of math for students who are learning disabled or differently-abled. There are several reasons for this.

- First, students are no longer manipulating concrete numbers; instead, they are working with letter representations of unknown quantities. Therefore, they must be able to recall math concepts and laws and their application. For example, it is easier for students to recall that 2×6 is the same as 6×2 (the commutative law of multiplication), than it is to remember that $xy = yx$. In the former case, the student can carry out the math or enter the numbers in a calculator to verify the truth of the statement. In the latter case, the student must recall the mathematical law and its proof, and apply it to unknown quantities represented by letters. For students who are concrete in their thought processes, the very symbolic nature of algebra puts them at a disadvantage.

- The vocabulary of algebra may be difficult for the LD students. They must learn terms such as polynomials, quadratic equations, linear equations, nonlinear equalities, and equivalencies.

- The nature of algebraic problems involves multiple steps. As a result, students are required to interpret the question, plan the solution, apply the concepts, sequence the steps, perform the operations, and recheck the answer, all of which require maximum attention and perseverance under conditions of test anxiety. Thus, for students to be successful in algebra, they need to know basic mathematic skills, terminology, symbolic representation, sequencing (steps required for problem solution), metacognition (self-monitoring), concentration, motivation, and persistence.

- Research studies have shown that a large number of LD students who have mastered math without difficulty in the elementary grades nevertheless struggle with algebra. In recognition of this, educators have developed a number of strategies in an attempt to make the symbolic nature of algebra more concrete. The majority of the strategies included below have been research-tested with LD populations and have been shown to improve the proficiency of LD students' performance on the types of algebra questions that appear on the SAT.

Self-Regulation Strategy

Similar to the Self-Questioning Strategy, the *Self-Regulation Strategy* is effective because it is generated by the student. Maccini and Hughes (1997) suggest the use of cue cards containing questions concerning representation ("Have I understood the question?") and solution ("Have I written an equation that includes all the information?"). In addition, a structured worksheet could be formulated that would help students focus on the solution of the problem by featuring the information that is known and unknown, the type of equation required, and the solution (Maccini and Gagnon, 2001). Here is an example of a structured worksheet.

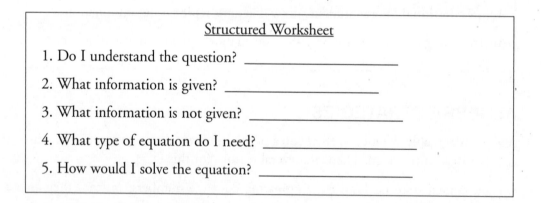

Structured Worksheet

1. Do I understand the question? _____
2. What information is given? _____
3. What information is not given? _____
4. What type of equation do I need? _____
5. How would I solve the equation? _____

An important part of the Self-Regulation Strategy is the *self-verbalization* component where students restate the question in their own words, picture the solution, talk through the solution, and check for errors. Thus, this strategy is effective for both the visual learner (using cue cards and visualizing the problem) and the auditory learner (restating the question and verbalizing the solution). Like all of the strategies, this strategy should be applied during practice sessions, and like the Self-Questioning Strategy mentioned earlier, the cue cards and worksheets should be phased out once the steps have been internalized.

Graphic Organizers

A graphic organizer is a means by which students can break down and solve problems by analyzing the information, categorizing it, and developing a plan for the solution to the problem through the use of a visual framework. Graphic organizers are used as a tool to assist students in reading comprehension and, more frequently, in organizing their writing. However, Ives and Hoy (2003) have discovered their applicability to higher level math. In their research, they have found that students with language processing and/or reading problems benefit from seeing information displayed in a visual framework.

In constructing a graphic organizer, the student would omit words, phrases, and sentences and include numbers or symbolic representations of numbers. The purpose of the graphic organizer in higher level math is not to learn, memorize, or reinforce basic math skills but to recognize patterns and concepts and to establish and reinforce the relationships between the math elements. Initially the student may require assistance constructing an organizer that effectively demonstrates the patterns the student wishes to represent visually. However, after this is modeled for the student and its effectiveness is demonstrated, the student can then proceed to take ownership of it and create a graphic organizer of his or her own.

The Ives and Hoy research (2003) includes an example of a graphic organizer used in solving linear equations with three variables.

III	II	I
$2x + 4y = 16$ $-2x - 3y + z = -5$ $2x + 2y - 3z = -3$	$\} \; x + 3z = 11$ $\} \; -y - 2z = -8$	$z = 3$
$2x + 4(2) + 2(3) = 16$ $2x + 14 + 16$ $2x = 2$ $x = 1$	$y + 3(3) = 11$ $y + 9 = 11$ $y = 2$	$z = 1$

Figure 14: Example of a Graphic Organizer

In the graphic organizer shown in Figure 14, three columns were created to represent each of the three variables. This particular frame was chosen because it best allows for the symbolic representation of the three elements. In this organizer, the top row was used to combine equations and eliminate variables until the value of one of the variables was reached. The purpose of the bottom row was to substitute values of the known variables until all the values were determined.

This is only one example of the use of a graphic organizer for solving algebraic equations. A single column organizer may be used for teaching values of exponents or square roots. As with most strategies, graphic organizers are tools. Students with graphomotor, or handwriting, problems may have difficulty constructing an organizer; therefore, this would not be an appropriate strategy for a student with this particular disability. However, as indicated above, graphic organizers may have great applicability for the student with language processing or reading problems because information can be displayed visually using a minimum of language.

Mnemonic Strategies

Mnemonic strategies are those designed to minimize memory retrieval by reducing concepts to a series of letters whereby each letter represents a larger idea. A large number of the strategies included in this book are in the form of mnemonics because, by recalling the sequence of letters, usually arranged to represent a common word, the individual is, in reality, recalling much more extensive information.

Researchers have found that LD students respond well to mnemonic strategies in math (Manalo et al, 2000) since the mnemonic stimulates memory retrieval and provides cues to problem-solving. There are some basic points to remember when using mnemonics. Students should understand

- What the purpose of the mnemonic is

- What each letter of the mnemonic stands for

- How it relates to the math problem

Initially, students should be provided with a cue card upon which is written both the mnemonic and what it means. Eventually the cue card will be discontinued. If you recall the mnemonic, *HOMES*, that you may have learned as a child to represent the Great Lakes (*H*uron, *O*ntario, *M*ichigan, *E*rie, *S*uperior), you will understand the effectiveness of mnemonic strategies in their ability to aid easy retrieval of information.

The DRAW Strategy

For students who have difficulty with the sequential aspect of solving equations, the *DRAW Strategy* (Mercer & Miller, 1992) is a cue that enables them to recall the steps involved. It may be used for the student who is just beginning to demonstrate proficiency in solving equations but has not yet internalized the steps or for students who suffer from test anxiety and require the mnemonic as a prompt.

Consider, for example, this problem: If the formula for the area of a square is represented by $A = 4s$, with s representing a side, what is the area of a square with a side of 4? The student applying the DRAW Strategy would first look to find the variable, which is s. Next, the student would read the equation and understand that what was needed was the substitution of the numerical value 4, for the variable s. If necessary, the student could draw the square, or just do the computation $4 \times 4 = 16$. The student would then check the answer and write it at the top of the column if the question is a grid-in or locate the answer among the choices if the question is a multiple-choice question.

DRAW Strategy

Discover the variable

Read the equation

Answer, or draw and check

Write the answer for the variable and check

The CAP Strategy

For students who have mastered the fundamentals of solving equations, the *CAP Strategy* (Mercer, 1994) is a further step in algebraic problem-solving. Students can use the DRAW Strategy to assist them in literally "drawing" or representing quantity in an equation; however, the CAP strategy is more abstract and its purpose is to cue students to recall the steps in a more sophisticated level of problem-solving.

For example, examine how the CAP Strategy can be applied to the following problem: The Junior class raised $360 from two plays and one car wash. The car wash raised $120 and one play earned twice what the other play did. How much did each play raise?

In this problem, the money each play raised (unknown) is represented by the letter x. The information is given that one play earned twice ($2x$) what the other (x) raised, and that the car wash raised $120. Translating this information into an equation, the student would have $2x + x + 120 = 360$. Following the first step of the CAP Strategy, the student would combine the $2x$ and x to equal $3x$. The student would then have the equation: $3x + 120 = 360$. The next step of the CAP strategy involves planning how to isolate the variable x. The student would then subtract the 120 from 360 leaving $3x = 240$. In order to isolate the variable, the student would have to divide both sides of the equation by 3, and would then be left with $x = 80$. However, this does not satisfy the problem. The third step of the CAP Strategy requires that the student put the value of the variable back into the problem in order to solve it. The questions asks, "How much did each play raise?" Accordingly, the student then finds that one play (x) raised $80 and the other ($2x$) raised $160. With the values the student found, it is possible to go back and recheck:

$$2x + x + 120 = 360$$
$$2(80) + (80) + 120 = 360$$
$$160 + 80 + 120 = 360$$
$$360 = 360$$

The student's answer is correct!

CAP Strategy

Combine like terms.

Ask yourself, "How can I isolate the variable?"

Put the value of the variable back in the original equation and check.

The STAR Strategy

Perhaps the best known and most researched mnemonic strategy with applications to algebra problem-solving and higher level math is the STAR Strategy (Maccini, McNaughton and Ruhl, 1999). Because STAR is a multistep strategy in which each step is broken down, it is best paired with a structured worksheet. Applying the principles of the C-R-A Strategy discussed earlier, it may be effective, when the STAR Strategy is introduced, to apply it to integers before applying the strategy to symbolic representations of numbers. Although there are only four steps to the STAR Strategy, each step has been broken down further. Initially the four letters plus the secondary question prompts should be written on a cue card; later, the four letters alone will suffice. Students will need time and repeated practice to master the STAR Strategy. It can be adapted to the concrete stage (manipulatives), the representational stage (student drawings), and finally, the abstract stage.

The main difference between the STAR Strategy and the CAP Strategy is that the STAR Strategy *with* the word prompts enables the student to work through each step of a multistep process. As the student becomes more proficient at setting up equations, applying the correct operation, carrying out the numeration, substituting the numbers into the equation for the answer, and finally rechecking, the process can be streamlined to either the four-step STAR Strategy or the three-step CAP Strategy.

STAR Strategy
Including the question prompts that relate to the **C-S-A Strategy**
(See "Word Problems Strategies" in this chapter.)

1. **Search** the word problem.
   (A) Read the problem carefully.
   (B) Ask yourself questions: "What facts do I know?" "What do I need to find?"
   (C) Write down facts.

2. **Translate** the words into a representation or an equation.
   (A) Choose a variable.
   (B) Identify the operation(s).
   (C) Represent the problem with manipulatives like beans or tiles (for a CONCRETE APPLICATION) **or**

   Draw a picture of the representation (REPRESENTATIONAL APPLICATION) **or**

   Write an algebraic equation (ABSTRACT APPLICATION).

3. **Answer** the problem.

4. **Review** the solution.
   (A) Reread the problem.
   (B) Answer question, "Does the answer make sense? Why?"
   (C) Check answer.

One final point requires mentioning: Perhaps because many LD students lack confidence, they tend to offer too much information. Often the solution to a math problem, particularly a geometry question, does not require the student to compute values for all variables, and the student who solves for all the variables is wasting time. As discussed, students need to underline or highlight what it is that needs to be solved and solve *only* what the question requires.

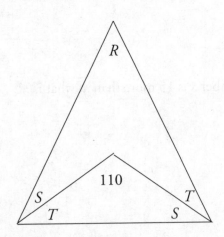

Figure 15

For example, the question states: In the above figure, what is the value of *R*?

(A) 60
(B) 50
(C) 70
(D) 40
(E) 30

Since there are 180° in a triangle, in order to find out the number of degrees in the two base angles, S and T, it is necessary to subtract the known angle, 110, from 180.

Therefore, $180 - 110 = 70$, so the sum of $S + T = 70$. Since each base angle of the larger triangle is $S + T$, the sum of the two base angles or $2(S + T) = 140$. Without solving for angles S and T, we now know that angle $R = 180 - 140$, or 40°. The question never required a solution for angle *S* and angle *T*, and, therefore, the student needs to underline the information in the question, "What is the value of *R*?"

As mentioned earlier, the strategies in this section are presented as tools to enable students with learning disabilities or learning differences who have studied the high school math curriculum and are familiar with the vocabulary of math to score optimally on the Math Section of the SAT. As a caution, not all the strategies are equally appropriate for all students. The degree of effectiveness of each of the strategies depends on each student's area of weakness, the ease with which each student is able to use the strategy, and the motivation of each student to use strategies. All strategies should be introduced prior to the day of testing. Students should select which, if any, of the strategies they might find helpful during a study session, and no strategy should be used on the SAT until the student is completely familiar with the strategy and feels comfortable applying it.

Application of Strategies

1. What is the perimeter of a triangle having two sides that are 8 inches in length and one angle that measures 60 degrees?

   (A) 16
   (B) 20
   (C) 24
   (D) 28
   (E) 36

2. If four times a number *x* is 15 more than *x*, what is *x*?

   (A) 3
   (B) 5
   (C) 9
   (D) 12
   (E) 15

3. An adult and three children went out to lunch. An adult meal cost $2.00 more than a child's meal. The total came to $50.00. What was the cost of the adult meal?

   (A) $8
   (B) $10
   (C) $12
   (D) $14
   (E) $16

4. Three brothers were born in consecutive years. The sum of the three birth years is 5973. Find the year in which the youngest brother was born.

   (A) 1988
   (B) 1989
   (C) 1990
   (D) 1991
   (E) 1992

5. A homeowner is building an enclosed rectangular play area in the back of his house with 76 feet of wooden fencing. The side of the play area next to the house will share a common 28 foot wall. What are the dimensions of the play area?

   (A) 76×28
   (B) 10×28
   (C) 12×28
   (D) 14×28
   (E) 24×28

6. A man runs a 100 foot cable off the top of a building to a point 60 feet from the base of the building. How tall is the building?

   (A) 80 feet
   (B) 90 feet
   (C) 100 feet
   (D) 110 feet
   (E) 120 feet

Answers and Strategies Applied

1. *Answer:* (C)

   Explanation: Using the geometry strategy, the study should apply the first step, self-questioning. What information is given? What information is necessary to answer the question? Do I know what a perimeter is? The next step is to draw a representation of a triangle, plugging in the information provided (Figure 16).

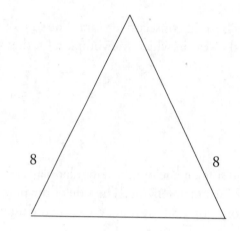

Figure 16: Example Using the Geometry Strategy

The next step is to do the calculation. Keeping in mind the fact that, since two sides measure 8, it must mean that another angle must also measure 60°. Therefore, 2(60) = 120, and subtracting 120 from 180 reveals that the final angle must also be 60°. If all angles are the same, all sides must be the same length. Therefore, the third side must also measure 8. However, the final step is to go back to the problem and locate what information it is asking for. The question requires the perimeter of the triangle. If all sides equal 8, the perimeter is 24 or choice (c).

2. *Answer:* (B)

   Explanation: To solve this algebra word problem, one could use the DRAW Strategy. In the first step of this strategy, we discover the variable (x). Next, we read the equation, "If four times a number x is 15 more than x, what is x?" Translating the words to an equation, we get

   $$4x = x + 15$$

   The next step tells us to answer the equation.

   $$4x = x + 15$$
   $$4x - x = x - x$$
   $$\frac{3x}{3} = \frac{15}{3}$$
   $$x = 5$$

   The final step is to write the answer in the equation and check.

   $$4(5) = (5) + 15$$
   $$20 = 20$$

   Therefore, according to our check, $x = 5$, and the answer is choice (b).

3. *Answer:* (D)

   Explanation: Demonstrating the use of the STAR Strategy (without the question prompts) with this algebra word problem, the first step requires that we search the word problem to determine the information that is required. The next step tells us to translate the words into an equation. The question states: "An adult and three children went out to lunch. An adult meal cost $2.00 more than a child's meal. The total came to $50.00. What is the cost of the adult meal?" If we designate the letter x to represent the cost of a child's meal, the equation would read

$$3(x) + x + 2 = 50$$

   The next step is to answer by doing the calculation.

$$4x + 2 = 50$$
$$4x + 2 - 2 = 50 - 2$$
$$\frac{4x}{4} = \frac{48}{4}$$
$$x = 12$$

   The last step in the STAR Strategy says to review the problem by rereading, answering, and checking. If we reread the problem, we see that the information required is the cost of the adult's, not the child's, meal. Since x represented a child's meal, and x was found to be $12, and the adult meal was $2 more than the child's meal, the adult's meal is $14 or choice (d). However, we must plug the numbers back into the equation to see if we are correct. Therefore,

$$4(12) + 2 = 50$$
$$48 + 2 = 50$$

4. *Answer:* (C)

   Explanation: The CAP Strategy would work well for this problem. The problem states: "Three brothers were born in consecutive years. The sum of the three birth years is 5973. Find the year in which the youngest brother was born." If we translate the question to an equation, the three consecutive birth years would become x, $x + 1$, and $x + 2$. The word "sum" is a clue that the three years must be added together and that the result would be 5973. Thus,

$$(x) + (x + 1) + (x + 2) = 5973$$

   According to the first step in the CAP Strategy, we must combine like terms. Therefore,

$$3x + 3 = 5973$$

   The next step is to ask ourselves if we can isolate the variable to solve the equation.

$$3x + 3 = 5973$$
$$3x + 3 - 3 = 5973 - 3$$
$$3x = 5970$$
$$\frac{3x}{3} = \frac{5970}{3}$$
$$x = 1990$$
$$x + 1 = 1991$$
$$x + 2 = 1992$$

The last step tells us to put the value of the variable(s) back in the problem and check.

$$(1990) + (1991) + (1992) = 1573$$

We have checked to determine that our computation is correct. However, the question does not ask us to solve the equation; it asks us to find the birth year of the youngest brother (x). The answer is therefore 1990 or choice (c).

5. *Answer:* (E)

   Explanation: Reading this question, we can see that we are asked to find dimensions, that is, length and width, of a play area. This, then, is a geometry problem. Therefore, we will once again use our Geometry Strategy. The first step is to self-question, or ask what the question is asking. As mentioned earlier, we are asked to find the dimensions of a play area. The next step is for us to draw the rectangular play area (Figure 17).

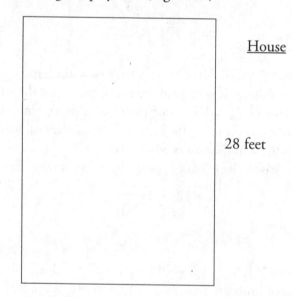

Figure 17: Example Using the Geometry Strategy

According to the problem, the homeowner has only 76 feet of fencing. One side of the play area will share a 28 foot common wall with the house. Since the shape is a rectangle, the opposite side will also be 28 feet long. The adjacent sides will be assigned x. The next step of the Geometry Strategy is to plug in the numbers. To do this, we must create an equation:

$$2x + 28 = 76$$

Next, we do the calculations that the strategy calls for and solve for x:

$$2x + 28 = 76$$
$$2x + 28 - 28 = 76 - 28$$
$$\frac{2x}{2} = \frac{48}{2}$$
$$x = 24$$

Next, we recheck by putting the value of x back into the equation:

$$2(24) + 28 = 76$$
$$48 + 28 = 76$$

Finally, we locate the information required by the problem. Once again, the question asks the dimensions of the play area. According to our solution, the dimensions are 24×28 or choice (e).

6. *Answer:* (a)

Explanation: Reading this word problem, we determine that the information required is the height of a building. However, the building is apparently one side of a triangle. Therefore, we must apply the Geometry Strategy. The first step is to self-question what information is necessary. We have performed this step and found that we are required to determine the height of a building which is, in fact, one side of a triangle. As we read the problem in order to perform the second step of the strategy, that is, to draw the triangle, we determine that the type of triangle is a right triangle. (See Figure 18.) The building is the vertical leg, the point at which the cable reaches 60 feet away is the horizontal leg, and the 100 foot cable from the top of the building to the point 60 feet from the base of the building is the hypotenuse. Since we have determined that the figure is that of a right triangle, we will need to find the formula of the Pythagorean Theorem at the beginning of the Math Section in order to solve for one of the legs.

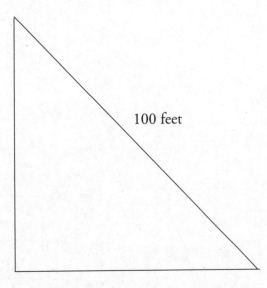

100 feet

Figure 18: Triangle Using the Geometry Strategy

The next step is to plug the numbers into the Pythagorean Theorem.

$$x^2 + (60)^2 = (100)^2$$
$$x^2 + 3600 = 10,000$$
$$x^2 + 3600 = 10,000 - 3600$$
$$x^2 = 6400$$
$$x = 80$$

The next step is to recheck the calculation:

$$(60)^2 + (80)^2 = (100)^2$$
$$3600 + 6400 = 10,000$$

Finally, we need to go back into the problem to determine the information that is required. The question asks: "How tall is the building?" Substituting our solution for x, the height of the building is 80 feet or choice (a).

Through repetition of specific text-taking strategies, students like Marisa can benefit on the Math section of the SAT.

Test-Taking Strategies

I've hated taking tests for as long as I can remember. When I was in first grade, I remember the teacher kept a chart on the wall. We had weekly spelling and reading tests, and we would get a gold star for every 100 we got on the tests. When we got ten stars, the teacher would give us a pencil with our name on it. At the end of the school year, most of the kids in my class had twenty or thirty pencils, something like that. I had one. I knew how to spell and how to read as good as the other kids, I think. But when the teacher gave out the white paper, I put the heading on the top of the page, and that's when I forgot everything. There is something about the word, "test" that makes me freeze up and makes my mind go blank. Maybe it's because I get nervous, huh?

Juan, a 16-year-old junior

HOW LEARNING DISABILITIES AFFECT GENERAL STUDENT PERFORMANCE ON THE SAT

Many students, ranging from LD to honor students, are plagued with test-taking anxiety. For some, the anxiety affects them in minor ways, perhaps nothing more than stomach "butterflies"; for others, the anxiety is so severe that they "freeze up" like Juan above, a situation referred to in an earlier chapter as cognitive paralysis. This chapter will delineate strategies that students can perform before, and possibly even during, the test to alleviate the problem of test-taking anxiety such as Juan describes.

What are the main problems LD students face on the SAT?

LD students face several problems on the SAT with regard to test-taking:

- Insufficient preparation

- Test anxiety

- Few, if any, test-taking strategies

- Inability to apply specific test-taking strategies as required

- Lack of time management strategies

What kind of test preparation is necessary?

First and foremost, students should study previous exams and/or sample exams. However, familiarity with the structure of the test is only the first step to success. The student must develop a good background in the content of the test. Full mastery of *all* the vocabulary or complete proficiency in *all* math concepts may be unrealistic, but certainly students should arrive at the testing situation feeling self-assured and confident with their level of advance preparation.

The most predictable parts of the SAT are the Math Section and the Identifying Sentence Errors, Improving Sentences, and Improving Paragraphs components of the Writing Section because these are based directly on the students' schoolwork since middle, if not elementary, school. There should be nothing completely unfamiliar about these sections, and this fact alone should alleviate some degree of test anxiety.

In preparation for the Math Section of the SAT, students should practice solving various problems in arithmetic, algebra, both basic and advanced, and geometry found in math review books, and, while doing so, they should identify those areas requiring additional practice. If specific areas of math continue to pose problems, the student should consult a review book or obtain tutorial help. In addition, although the math concepts may be familiar, the wording of problems may pose difficulty. For this reason, the student should become familiar with Appendix B, "Signal Words in Math."

In preparation for the Improving Sentences, Identifying Sentence Errors, and Improving Paragraphs components of the Writing Section, students should familiarize themselves with the strategies presented in the Writing Section chapter of this book (Chapter 3), as well as with the rules of grammar and correct written English. At the point where students feel reasonably confident, they should attempt sample questions to assess their proficiency and pinpoint areas that require additional study.

The remainder of this chapter will discuss:

- Strategies for specific types of test questions

- General test-taking strategies

- Ways to alleviate test-anxiety

- Time management

GENERAL TEST-TAKING STRATEGIES

Over the years, researchers and practitioners in the field of special education have observed that LD students do not perform optimally on standardized tests. One reason appears to be that LD students lack sufficient test-taking strategies. As a result, strategies have been developed to improve students' scores and enable LD students to demonstrate what they know.

One technique that Carman and Adams (1972) developed to help students prepare for tests is the *SCORER technique.* According to this method, students would preview the test to assess the time demands. Hopefully, in preparation for the SAT, students would note the time allotted for each section and their individual testing modifications (i.e., 50 percent additional time, 100 percent additional time). For example, if the critical reading section allotted 25 minutes to complete 25 questions, a student permitted 100 percent additional time, or double time, would be permitted 50 minutes. This testing modification applies to all sections of the SAT.

In addition, the SCORER technique reminds students to be aware of cue words. Students should take note of absolute words like, "all," "none," and "never" because these are rarely found in correct choices. In addition, students should be prepared to omit difficult questions. On sentence completion and on math questions, the easier questions appear at the beginning of the section with the questions getting progressively more difficult. As a result, students proceed until the level of difficulty exceeds their ability and they are guessing at the answers. However, on passage-based reading and on the English section—Improving Sentences, Identifying Sentence Errors, and Improving Paragraphs—the difficulty level is *not* progressive, and students must decide what questions are too difficult and should be omitted.

According to the SCORER technique, students must read all directions and examples carefully and completely. Having taken practice exams prior to the actual SAT, students should be familiar with the wording of the directions and examples. However, reading and rereading questions is a necessity and should become a necessary step in any test-taking strategy.

As indicated in Chapter 4, students need to review the skill of estimation to see if their answers fall within a realistic range. For example, if a question calls for students to determine how much to pay for an item marked $19.59 that is on sale for 20 percent off the listed price, the student should determine that 20 percent = 1/5 and, since $19.59 is close to $20.00, the sale price can be estimated to be $4.00 off, or in the range of $15.00 to $16.00.

Finally, although students must review their answers, they should be particularly cautious about changing answers.

The SCORER Technique

Schedule your time

Cue words

Omit or set aside difficult questions

Read directions and examples carefully

Estimate the possible range of answers

Review answers

SPECIFIC TEST-TAKING STRATEGIES

Clues for Answering Multiple-Choice Questions

Strichart and Mangrum (1993) suggest some general clues that LD students may find helpful when answering multiple-choice questions. However, students should be aware that the following are clues, *not* hard-and-fast rules and, therefore, should be used judiciously. Students should pay particular attention when

1. An answer choice contains an *absolute word* such as "all," "none," "always," or "never" because these choices are rarely correct
2. An answer choice contains a *qualifying word* such as "most," "some," "several," "many," or a "few" because these choices are frequently correct
3. There are two answer choices that are *opposite* because it is likely that one of them will contain the answer
4. There are two answer choices that are *very similar* because, as a rule, neither one is likely to be the correct choice
5. The answer choice contains *the most technical* language because it is likely to be the correct answer
6. The answer choice that contains the *most general* or **most familiar** language, or the *longest* and *most complete* answer because it is likely to be the correct choice
7. One of the choices is **"all of the above"** because more than likely it is the correct answer

Once again, these are general hints for answering multiple-choice questions and *should be used with caution*.

The 5-L Strategy for Guessing

Since the SAT is a penalty test, that is, there is a penalty for guessing, students need guidelines to help them decide when to guess and when not to guess. The *5-L Strategy* is designed to provide students with general rules for guessing. According to this strategy, students should first *look* at all the choices in a multiple-choice question. Next, students should *leave out*, or eliminate, all obviously incorrect answers. Students should then *look back* at the question to see if any answers can be eliminated or to see if choices can be narrowed further. Students should *lean toward* answering all questions involving interpretation of charts, graphs, maps, or pictures since a careful examination will usually yield the answer. Finally, students should *look* for patterns in the answers; for example, rarely, on multiple-choice tests, will there be five (a) choices in a row. Therefore, students who find that, in guessing, most of their choices are (c), need to review the questions.

These are general "guess guidelines" to give a student an idea of when to and when not to guess. The best rule, however, is still the *50/50 rule*; if students can eliminate all choices but two, giving them a 50/50 chance of getting the correct answer, then it pays for them to guess.

The 5-L Strategy for Guessing

Look at all choices

Leave out obviously incorrect answers

Look back at the question

Lean toward answering questions with charts, graphs, tables

Look for patterns in answers

The SPLASH Strategy

Strategies for multiple-choice types of tests do not differ dramatically from general test-taking strategies; there are some specific steps students may want to take.

A test-taking strategy was developed by Simmonds et al. (1989) to assist LD students to focus on the necessary test-taking skills for multiple-choice tests. Using the acronym, SPLASH, students will remember that they must first *skim* the entire test, or in the case of the SAT, the section, in order to formulate a plan for attacking the test. For example, in those sections, like passage-based reading, where questions are random and not in ascending order of difficulty, students may make a preliminary decision about which questions they may, perhaps, wish to eliminate.

Next, having previewed the section, students may *plan* their strategy. Working within their time restraints, students may decide to answer the easiest questions first, working toward the more challenging questions. As they answer progressively more difficult questions, the students must choose the questions to *leave out* altogether. As mentioned earlier, students should *attack* the questions they know immediately and *systematically guess* on those questions they feel they may have a possibility of getting correct. Finally, students should leave 5 to 10 percent of their time for *house cleaning*, that is, reviewing their tests to make certain they have filled in all answers, cleaned up erasures completely, and checked computer forms.

Using a systematic test-taking strategy can dramatically improve students' scores and alleviate test anxiety.

The SPLASH Strategy

Skim the test

Plan a strategy

Leave out tough questions

Attack questions you know

Systematically guess

House cleaning

The RISEN Strategy for Multiple-Choice Tests

Like the SPLASH Strategy, the RISEN Strategy addresses multiple-choice types of questions and gives students a systematic and structured test-taking approach.

With the *RISEN Strategy*, as with any test strategy, the student should first *read* the question. While doing this, the student is becoming familiar with the vocabulary and is underlining key words, which may give clues to the answer. Next, the student should begin eliminating obviously *incorrect* answers. If one choice remains, that is the answer the student will *select*. However, if more than one choice remains, the student must reread the choices again. Finally, after the student has selected a choice, *no answer* should be changed.

Although the following example is not on the same level of difficulty as an SAT question, it will help explain the strategy:

Only one continent is an island, and it is

1. North America
2. Africa
3. Australia
4. Hawaii

The student would first read the question to access his or her background information on geography and the continents. Next, the student would eliminate the most obviously incorrect answer, Hawaii, because it is not a continent. Three choices remain so the student would reread the choices carefully. Having done so, the student can eliminate North America and Africa because they are not islands. The correct choice would thus be (3) Australia. The student, having made this choice, would not change it.

The RISEN Strategy

Read all choices

Incorrect choices should be eliminated

Select the last choice if only one remains

Each choice should be reread if more than one remains

Never change an answer

STARS Strategy for Answering Sentence Completion Tests

Note: Specific strategies for answering Sentence Completions can also be found in Chapter 2.

In a Sentence Completion Test, students are required to fill in words in a sentence that have been omitted. The choices are presented in the form of multiple-choice questions; therefore, in addition to specific steps in the sentence completion strategy, students can apply the RISEN Strategy as well.

In the **STARS Strategy** the student would first read the sentence, thinking of what it is saying. Next, the student would ask, "What information is missing?" The student would then reread the sentence with the answer choice to see if it makes sense.

Below is an example of a sentence for purposes of explanation that is far easier than a student would normally find on the actual SAT:

Good _____ celebrate their freedom by voting on Election Day.

1. friends
2. citizens
3. neighbors
4. Republicans

Reading the sentence, the student would decide whether or not the vocabulary is clear and would look to underline key words. The key word in this example is "voting." Next, the student would think about what the sentence is saying—some people celebrate their freedom by voting. The student determines that the name of the specific group is the information that is missing. If voting is the key word, the student can eliminate friends and neighbors. Republicans, too, can be eliminated as being too specific. If the student fills in the word "citizens," the sentence would then read: "Good citizens celebrate their freedom by voting on Election Day." The student would, thus, determine that the choice "citizens" makes sense in the context of the sentence.

The STARS Strategy

Scan statement

Think of what it is saying

Ask what is missing

Reread the sentence with your answer

See if it makes sense

Strategies for Essay Tests

Essay tests require different test-taking skills than multiple-choice tests. Although thinking through the question is an essential element in both, it becomes paramount to success on essay tests. A key strategy for essay tests with which students should familiarize themselves is the *POWER(R) Strategy*—a mnemonic for plan, organize, write, edit, revise (reread)—which provides students with a systematic approach to essay-writing tasks. (See Chapter 3.)

In addition, Alley and Deshler (1979) emphasized the need for students to study direction words. They made the observation that often the failure of LD students to understand the meaning of direction words on essay tests impedes optimal performance. As such, by way of preparation, students should study the following direction words and their meanings:

- Compare—This direction word indicates that the student must find similarities between the two or more things that are being compared.

- Contrast—This direction word indicates that the student must find differences between the two or more things that are being contrasted.

- Discuss, describe, and explain—These direction words request that the student write a complete and thorough examination of the subject. When students encounter these test directions, they should write everything they know about the subject, and they should use brainstorming as a prewriting strategy.

- Criticize, evaluate—These direction words indicate that the student is to arrive at a judgment about the subject based on an examination of both the positive and negative aspects.

- Justify—This direction word indicates the need for the student to write a persuasive essay in which he or she provides evidence to support a particular action or decision.

- Trace—This direction word indicate the need for students to follow a sequential order of events.

- Relate—This direction word directs the student to discuss or explain how or why two events are related.

- Summarize—This direction word directs the student to discuss only the main points about the subject(s).

- Diagram, illustrate—These direction words direct the student to create a drawing. It is unlikely that these direction words will appear on the SAT.

ONE FINAL DETAIL STUDENTS NEED TO REMEMBER ABOUT ESSAY TESTS

No matter how brilliant or well-written their essays, if students do not address the question, they will be receiving a minimal grade. Similarly, if their essays take the form of elongated summaries and fail to take a position, students will *not* receive an optimal grade.

TEST ANXIETY

Along with poor test-taking strategies, text anxiety is perhaps the most serious problem for LD students, if not most students, taking the SAT. When students fall victim to test anxiety, they will have problems with memory, planning, organization, time management (and test completion), and even the test-taking strategies they have practiced. As a result, they will not achieve an optimal score.

First of all, what is test anxiety? Test anxiety is the apprehension or fear students feel before taking an exam. Most students taking a test as important as the SAT will experience some degree of test anxiety; however, in its worst form, test anxiety can lead to migraine headaches, vomiting, dizziness, severe depression, panic, and "freezing," a form of mental paralysis that leaves victims unable to proceed with testing.

Some general symptoms of test anxiety are

- Stomach "butterflies"

- Sweaty palms

- Rapid heartbeat

- Rapid breathing

Experts say that mild symptoms like the above are, in themselves, not detrimental. In fact, they often signal an "adrenaline rush" that may actually promote sharper thinking. However, since test anxiety is nothing more than a fear of failure, there are steps students can take to keep test anxiety in check.

1. *Practice*—Students who have taken sample tests and are familiar with test format, directions, and time allotment will be less likely to succumb to test anxiety.
2. *Plan*—Students who have structured test-taking strategies to help themselves plan how to address the SAT will feel more relaxed about it.

3. *Prepare in advance*—Students who study math, word structures, and grammar rules will be more optimistic about their performance and less apt to fall victim to test anxiety.

4. *Make positive self-statements*—Knowing they are well prepared, students should make positive self-statements and visualize themselves getting exceptional scores.

5. *Destress*—Students should not reflect on any other issues besides taking the SAT; problems with family, money, dates, or friends should be left behind and should not accompany students to the test.

6. *Reduce pressure*—Students can reduce pressure on themselves by understanding that the results of the SAT, although important, are only one factor in the college admission process. Furthermore, they can take the SAT several times and can cancel the results of any SAT they have taken.

Relaxation Techniques

There are a number of relaxation techniques students can use both prior to and during the SAT to help alleviate test anxiety. As they are sitting in the testing room waiting to receive their exams, students should take the opportunity to close their eyes, concentrate on breathing in and out. Next, they should try to block out the sounds and commotion around them by imagining a quiet, tranquil, picturesque place—perhaps a solitary beach or a babbling brook—and, while *visualizing* the serenity of the location, they should concentrate on feeling each muscle group relax. Students will feel infinitely calmer after just a minute or two of this type of relaxation.

Another form of quick relaxation involves the *tightening and releasing of the muscles*. Students would first tighten the muscles of their toes, holding that for a count of ten and relax their toes. Feeling the release of tension, they would then flex the muscles of their feet, again holding the tension for a count of ten, and then relax. Students would then slowly move up through their bodies—first the muscles in the legs, next the abdomen, back, neck, and face—concentrating on contacting and relaxing the muscles for a quick release of tension. As they flex and relax their muscles, they are breathing slowly and deeply.

Speaking of breathing, there is a relaxation technique that involves *alternate nostril breathing*. First, the right nostril is closed by the student applying pressure with the right thumb, and the student inhales through the left nostril. This is done to a 4-second count. Then, the left nostril is closed by closing it off with the right ring finger and the pinky, and, simultaneously the pressure is removed from the right nostril, through which the student exhales. This is done for 8 seconds. Next, the student inhales through the right nostril for 4 seconds, closes the right nostril with the right thumb, and exhales through the left nostril for 8 seconds. The purpose of alternate nostril breathing is that it produces maximum function to both sides of the brain, the left containing logical, analytical function, and the right containing creative function. Because students need whole-brain function, not to mention relaxation, to perform optimally on the SAT, this would appear to be a beneficial technique.

TIME MANAGEMENT

During practice, students need to note how much time is allotted for each section, taking into account their own individual testing modifications (i.e., an additional 50 or 100 percent). As they become more proficient and more comfortable with the format of the SAT, students should take all practice exams with the same time constraints as they will have during the actual exam. If they are repeatedly unable to complete a section within the allotted time frame, students must develop a strategy to help them do so.

This strategy may include

- Previewing the section

- Using a 60-second timer per question

- Answering the easiest questions first

- Using strategies to eliminate questions

- Placing stars before questions students will come back to

- Checking time spent on one question (if students feel they have persevered too much on a single question)

Through test preparation and practice, students should be able to work out time management problems; however, if, during the test, students become fearful that they are running out of time and begin to panic, they should put the pen down, take a few deep breaths, shut their eyes, clear their minds, clench and unclench their fists, and begin once again with a positive outlook. Most important of all, students *must* learn to ignore the movement of other students; completing the test early does not indicate high scores.

Should students find they have *extra time* on a particular section, they should

1. Make sure they have *completed* all questions they wanted to complete
2. *Recheck* questions for comprehension; that is, to see if they have read and interpreted the question correctly
3. *Look over* the omitted questions again and try using the 5-L Strategy for Guessing
4. Keep in mind that *no answers should be changed* unless students have inadvertently chosen the wrong answer or have misread the question
5. *Recheck* the answer sheet for incomplete or incorrect information or omissions
6. Make sure all *erasures* are complete and all answers are legible
7. Recheck personal *identification* information (name, date, testing center code)

SAT TEST DAY

Although there are a number of steps the student can take the morning and day of the SAT, preparation really begins the night before. A few minutes of advance preparation the night before the SAT will allow the student to wake up relaxed.

The Night Before the SAT

Students should

- Organize photo identification and testing admission materials

- Organize testing supplies—several pencils, pens, calculator (with extra batteries), a watch

- Recheck testing center and time

- Check public transportation schedules or gasoline if they or their parents are driving

- Lay out comfortable clothing and shoes

- Pack "munchies," like gum, mints, or snack bars, water, and tissues

The Day of the SAT

Students *should*

- Eat a light breakfast or bring along a cereal or protein bar

- Destress by reading, taking a TV break, listening to music, or walking

- Bring everything they organized the night before

- Listen to the proctor's instructions

- Think positive

Students should *avoid*

- Negative thoughts

- Attempting to predict the difficulty of the SAT

- Speaking to other students about the exam before the exam

- Reflecting about omissions in preparation or problems they encountered in practice

- Comparing notes with other students after the exam

Above all, students like Juan need to be reminded that the future course of their lives is *not* dependent on the results of this one exam, and they have the opportunity to take the SAT multiple times if they are not pleased with the results.

Index of Strategies

Appendix A: Prefixes, Suffixes, and Roots

Prefixes	Meanings	Examples
a-	not, without	amoral, apolitical
ab-	away from	absent, abstain
ad-	to, toward, again	addict, addition
ante-	before	antecedent, antebellum
anti-	against	anticlimax, antisocial
arch-	chief	archbishop
auto-	self	autobiography
be-	to become, cause	bedevil, befriend
bi-	two	bicycle, bisect
circum-	around	circumscribe
co-	together	costar, copilot
com-	together	compose, compress
con-	with, together	conjoin, construct
contra-	against	contradict, contrast
counter-	in opposition	counterfeit
de-	down, away from	deplane, descent
demi-	half	demitasse, demigod
dia-	across, through	diameter, dialogue
dis-	opposite, reverse	disagree, disband
dys-	not, not normal	dyslexia, dysfunction
en- (or *em-*)	to cause, put into or on	enable, enmesh
epi-	add on, against, to	epidemic, epilogue
equi-	equal	equidistant, equilateral
ethno-	race, nation	ethnic, ethnology
ex-	out, up, away, completely	exit, expand
extra-	outside, beyond	extracurricular
fore-	previously	forecast, forefront
hemi-	half	hemisphere
hydro-	water	hydroelectric
hyper-	beyond, over	hyperactive
hypo-	under, below	hypodermic
il-	not	illegible, illiterate
im-, *in-*	not	impossible, inactive
infra-	below	infrastructure

Prefixes	Meanings	Examples
inter-	between	interact, intervene
intra-	within, inside	intramural
intro-	in, into	introduce, introspect
ir-	not	irregular, irresistible
iso-	equal	isosceles, isotherm
mal-	bad	malady, maladroit
meta-	change	metamorphosis
micro-	small	microphone
mid-	in the middle	midterm, midway
mini-	small	miniature, miniskirt
mis-	poorly, badly	misprint, mistake
multi-	many	multimedia, multiply
neo-	new	Neolithic, neophyte
non-	not, against	nonconformist
ob-, oc-, of-, op-	blocking, in the way	object, obstruct
omni-	all	omnipotent
out-	exceeding, external	outperform, outreach
over-	excessively, upper, outer	overjoyed, overcoat
pan-	all, whole	pandemic, panorama
para-	with, similar	parallel, paralegal
per-	through	perforate, percussion
peri-	all around, about	perimeter, peripheral
poly-	many	polygamy, polygon
post-	after	postgraduate, postwar
pre-	before	precede, predict
pro-	for, in favor of, before	proponent, prologue
proto-	earliest, first	prototype, protoplasm
pseudo-	false	pseudonym
re-	back, again	repaint, reread
retro-	backward	retrogress, retrospect
semi-	half	semicircle, semicolon
sub-	under	submerge, submarine
super-	more than, above, over	superhighway
tele-	far	telescope, telephone
trans-	across	transform, transact
ultra-	beyond	ultramodern
un-	not, reversal	unhappy, unaware
under-	beneath, not enough	underground
up-	upper, upward	uphold, upheaval

Number Prefixes

Prefixes	Meanings	Examples
uni-	one	uniform, unicycle
mono-	one	monocle, monotone
bi-	two	bicycle, bilateral
duo-	two	dual, duet
tri-	three	triangle, tricycle
quad-	four	quadrant, quadruplet
tetra-	four	tetrameter
quint-	five	quintet, quintuplet
pent-	five	pentagon, pentameter
sex-	six	sextet, sextuplet
hex-	six	hexagon, hexameter
sept-	seven	septuplet
hept-	seven	heptameter
oct-	eight	octagon, octane
nov-	nine	novena
dec-	ten	decade, decathlon
cent-	hundred	centimeter, centipede
milli-	thousand	millennium

Suffixes

Suffixes	Meanings	Examples
-able, -ible	capable of, worthy	comfortable
-age	act of, state of	bondage, luggage
-acy, -isy	quality	hypocrisy, piracy
-al, -eal, -ial	related to, action of	denial, arrival, aboreal
-ance, -ence	act of, state of	allowance
-ant	one who	defendant, accountant
-er, -or	agent, one who	author, teacher
-ed	past tense	cooked, jumped
-ery	place to practice, condition	bravery, surgery
-dom	condition or state of	wisdom, kingdom
-ent	having the quality of	reverent, different
-en	made of, to make	darken, sadden
-eur, -er, -or	one who	peddler, worker
-er	degree of comparison	better, fairer
-est	degree of comparison	smartest, fairest
-ful, -full	of	restful, faithful
-hood	state of being	boyhood
-ile, -il	capable of being	docile
-ier, -ior	one who	warrior, carrier
-ify	to make	beautify, magnify
-ic, -ical	like, made of	toxic, historical
-ing	action of	jumping, sitting
-ion	state of	intoxication, action
-ism	fact of being	Taoism, socialism
-ish	like	squeamish, foolish
-ist	a person who does	artist, scientist

Suffixes	Meanings	Examples
-ity, -ty	state of	beauty, humanity
-itis	inflammation of	tonsillitis, appendicitis
-ive	having nature of	active, pensive
-ize	to make	hypnotize, familiarize
-less	without	penniless, careless
-let	small	starlet, hamlet
-ly	like, happening	weekly, sadly
-ment	state of, quality, act of	merriment, movement
-meter	measuring implement	thermometer
-ness	state of	kindness, happiness
-ology	study of	biology, geology
-ous, -lous	full of	perilous, joyous
-ship	quality or state of	friendship, leadership
-scope	instrument for seeing	periscope, microscope
-some	like	tiresome, wholesome
-tion, -sion	state or act of	construction, action
-ty	quality or state of	liberty, beauty
-ward	to, toward	inward, forward
-wise	in a manner	likewise, clockwise
-y	like, full of, small	kitty, noisy

Word Roots

Roots	Meanings	Examples
acro	height, top, beginning	acrobat, acronym
aero	air	aerate, aerospace
agr(i)	farming	agriculture, agrarian
alter	other	altercation, alteration
ambi/amphi	both, around	ambidextrous
ambul	walk, move	amble, ambulate
ami/amo	love	amiable, amity
ang	bend	angle, angular
ana	back, against, again	anachronism, analysis
anim	spirit, life	animate, animal
ann, enn	year	anniversary
anthropo	human	anthropology
apt, ept	fasten	aptitude, inept
aqua	water	aquatic, aquarium
arch(a)(i)	primitive	archaeology, archaic
art	skill	artist, artisan
astro, aster	star	astronomy, asteroid
aud(i)(io)	hear	audible, audience
bar(o)	pressure	barometer, isobar
bell(i)	war	belligerent, bellicose
bene	good, well	beneficial, benefactor
biblio	books	bibliography, bible
bio	life	biography, biology
brev	short	brevity, abbreviation
cam	field	campaign, campus

Roots	Meanings	Examples
capt	head	captain, capture
cardi(o)	heart	cardiac, cardiology
carn(i)	flesh, meat	carnal, carnivorous
cata	down, against	catacomb, catalog
caust, caut	burn	caustic, cauterize
cede, ceed	go, yield	proceed, recede
ceive, cept	take	accept, receive
celer	fast	accelerate, decelerate
centr	center	central, centrifuge
cephalo	head	encephalitis, cephalic
cerebr(o)	brain	cerebral, cerebrum
cert	sure	certain, certificate
cess	go, yield	recession, cessation
chrom	color, pigment	chromatic, chromium
chron(o)	time	chronic, synchronize
cide, cise	cut, kill	excise, suicide
claim, clam	shout	exclaim, clamor
clar	clear	clarify, declaration
cline	lean	recline, inclination
cogn	know	recognize, cognition
commun	common	community, commune
corp(o)	body	corporation, corpse
cosm(o)	universe	cosmic, microcosm
cranio	skull	cranium, cranial
crat	rule	democrat, bureaucrat
cred	believe	credit, incredible
crypt(o)	hidden, secret	crypt, cryptic
cumul	mass, heap	accumulate
cycl	circle, ring	bicycle, cyclone
dem	people	democracy, epidemic
derm	skin	epidermis, dermatitis
dict	speak	dictation, predict
div	separate	divide, dividend
domin	master	dominate, dominion
don(at)	give	donate, pardon
duc(t)	lead	aqueduct, educate
dur	harden, lasting	durable, endurance
dyn(am)	power, energy	dynamic, dynamite
esth, aesth	feeling, sensation	aesthetic, kinesthetic
eu	good, well	euphonic
fac(t)	make, do	factory, manufacture
fer	bear, bring, carry	ferry, transfer
fid	faith	fidelity, confide
firm	strong	affirm, confirm
flect, flex	bend	deflect, flexible
flor(a)	flower	floral, florist
form	shape	conform, uniform
fract, frag	break	fragile, fracture
fug	flee, escape	fugitive, refugee
funct	perform, work	function, defunct
gen	birth, race	genesis, generate
geo	earth	geography, geology
gon	angle	octagon, polygon

Roots	Meanings	Examples
grad	step, stage	gradual, graduate
gram	letter, written	diagram, grammar
graph(y)	write	autograph, biography
grat	pleasing	grateful, gratuity
gress	to step	egress, regression
hab, hib	hold	inhabit, prohibit
heter(o)	different	heterogeneous
hom(o)	alike	homogenize
hydr	water	hydrant, hydration
icon(o)	image	icon, iconoclast
idio	peculiar, distinct	idiot, idiom
imag	likeness	image, imaginary
init	beginning	initial, initiation
integ	whole	integral, integrate
ject	throw	eject, project
jud, jur, jus	law	judge, jury, justice
junct	joint	conjunction, juncture
juven	young	juvenile, rejuvenate
kine	motion	kinetic, telekinesis
lab	work	collaborate
laps	slip	elapse, relapse
lex	words, reading	dyslexia, lexicon
liber	free	liberate, liberty
loc	place	dislocate, location
log(o), logy	word	analogy, logic
loqu, locu	speak	eloquent, elocution
luc	light	elucidate, lucid
lud, lus	play	delude, illusion
lum(in)	light	illuminate
luna	moon	lunar, lunatic
man	hand	maneuver, manipulate
mand	order	command, demand
mania	madness	egomania, maniac
mar	sea	marine, maritime
mars, mart	warlike	martial, martinet
mater, matr	mother	maternal, matrimony
mech	machine	mechanic
medi	middle	mediocre, medium
mem(or)	remember	commemorate
mens, ment	mind	demented, mental
merge, mers	dip into, dive	immerse, submerge
migr	depart, move	immigrant, migrate
miss, mit	send	dismiss, emit
mob	move	immobile, mobility
mon	warn	admonish, monitor
morph	form	amorphous
mort	death	immortal, mortuary
mot, mov	move	demote, remove
mut	change	mutation, mutant
narr	tell	narrative, narrator
nat	born	nation, natural
nav	ship	navigate, navy
nom(in)	name	misnomer, nominal
not	mark	denote, notable

Roots	Meanings	Examples
nov	new	innovation, renovate
noun, nun	declare	announce, enunciate
num(er)	number	enumerate, numerous
ocu	eye	binocular, oculist
op(t)	visible	autopsy, optic
opt	best	optimal, optimist
orig	beginning	aborigine, originate
pater, part	father	paternal, patriarch
path	feeling	empathy, pathetic
ped	foot	pedal, pedestrian
pel, pul	drive, force, urge	compel, expulsion
pend	hang	pendant, suspend
phil	love, friend	bibliophile
phon	sound	microphone, phonics
photo	light	photogenic
phys	nature, the body	physical, physician
pod	foot	podiatrist, podium
poli	city	metropolis, politics
pop	people	popular, population
port	carry	import, portable
psych	mind, mental	psyche, psychology
put	think	computer, deputy
ques	ask, seek	question, request
radi(c)	root	eradicate, radical
rect	straight	erect, direction
rid	laugh	deride, ridiculous
rupt	break	disruption, interrupt
san	health	sane, sanitary
scend	climb	ascend, transcend
sci	know	omniscient, science
scop	see	microscope, telescope
scribe	write	describe, transcribe
script	written	description, script
se	apart	secede, seclude
sect	cut	bisect, intersection
sed	settle	sedate, sedentary
sens	feel	sense, sensitive
serv	save, keep	conservation, preserve
sign	mark	insignia, signature
sim	like	similarity, simile
sol	alone	desolate, solitary
sol	sun	solar, solarium
solv	loosen	absolve, resolve
somn	sleep	insomnia, somnolent
son	sound	resonant, sonar
soph	wise	philosopher
spec(t)	see	inspect, spectacle
spir	breathe	inspire, respiration
sta	stand	stable, static
stell	star	constellation, stellar
strict	tighten	constrict, restriction
struct	build	construct, instruction
sum	highest	summary, summit
tact, tang	touch	contact, tangible

Roots	Meanings	Examples
tax	arrangement	syntax, taxonomy
tech(no)	skill	technique, technology
temp(or)	time	contemporary
ten	hold	tenant, tenure
term(in)	end	determine, terminal
terr	land	terrace, territory
the(o)	god	monotheism, theology
therm	heat	thermal, thermostat
tort	twist	contortion, retort
tox	poison	intoxicate, toxin
tract	pull, drag	attract, tractable
trib	give	attribute, contribution
turb	confusion	disturbance, turbulent
urb	city	suburb, urban
vac	empty	evacuate, vacation
vag	wander	vagrant, vague
var	different	variety, various
ven	come	convention, intervene
ver	truth	veracity, verdict
verb	word	verbalize, verbose
vers, vert	turn	invert, reverse
vic	conquer	conviction, victory
vid	see	evidence, video
viv	life, live	vivacious, revival
voc	voice	advocate, vocalize
void	empty	avoid, void
vol	wish, will	benevolent, voluntary
volv	roll	involve, revolve
vor	eat	carnivorous

Appendix B: Signal Words in Math

SIGNAL WORDS FOR ADDITION

- total
- sum
- increased by
- plus
- more than
- added (to)
- greater (than)
- combined (together)
- together
- total (of)
- added (to)
- specific examples: older than, farther than, consecutive

Examples of Algebraic Word Problems Using Addition

The **sum** of the sides of a triangle is 45.	$s + s + s = 45$
The length of the room is 6 feet **more** than the width.	$l = w + 6$
Ellen is 8 years **older than** Jane.	$e = j + 8$
The **total** weight of my two dogs is 50 pounds.	$x + y = 50$
Six **added to** a number x is 32.	$x + 6 = 32$

SIGNAL WORDS FOR SUBTRACTION

- less (than)

- fewer (than)

- minus

- decreased (by)

- difference (between)

- difference (of)

- subtracted (from)

- reduced (by)

- diminished (by)

- specific examples: younger than, lighter than, shorter than

Examples of Algebraic Word Problems Using Subtraction

John is 4 years **younger than** Mary.	$j = m - 4$
There are 10 **fewer** children in Bill's class than Jim's.	$b = j - 10$
In the new carton, broken eggs were **reduced by** 3.	$n = b - 3$
The **difference between** my weight and yours is 4 pounds.	$m - y = 4$
Nine **less than** the number x is 21.	$x - 9 = 21$

SIGNAL WORDS FOR MULTIPLICATION

- times

- multiplied (by)

- product (of)

- of

- specific examples: double, triple, twice, two or three (or more) times

Examples of Algebraic Word Problems Using Multiplication

The length **times** the width is 16.	$lw = 16$
The **product of** the ages of the triplets was 18.	$3t = 18$
When x is **multiplied** by 3 the answer is 15.	$3x = 15$
One quarter **of** the students were invited to the party.	$p = (1/4)x$
Twice a number x is 46.	$2x = 46$

SIGNAL WORDS FOR DIVISION

- divided by

- divided into

- quotient (of)

- per

- out of

- into

- specific examples: ratio (of), average (of), percent (of), rate (of)

Examples of Algebraic Word Problems Using Division

The length **divided by** the width is 10.
$l/w = 10$ or $l \div w = 10$

The **quotient of** x and 4 is 12.
$x/4 = 12$ or $x \div 4 = 12$

If I travel 180 miles in 3 hours, what is my
rate of speed?
$r = 180/3$ or $r = 180 \div 3$

The **average of** my 3 test grades is 90.
$$\frac{a + b + c}{3} = 90$$

What is the cost **per** pencil if x pencils cost
48 cents?
$p = 48/x$ or $p = 48 \div x$

FACTS ABOUT EXPONENTS

- Any number (except 0) raised to the power of zero is equal to 1
  Example: $174^0 = 1$

- Any number raised to the first power is always equal to itself.
  Example: $8^1 = 8$

- If a number is raised to the second power, it is said to be squared.
  Example: $3^2 = 3 \times 3 = 9$

- If a number is raised to the third power, it is said to be cubed.
  Example: $4^3 = 4 \times 4 \times 4 = 64$

ORDER OF OPERATIONS-PEMDAS

In evaluating algebraic expressions, remember the order of operations by the phrase:

Please Excuse My Dear Aunt Sally

Parenthesis
Exponents
Multiplication
Division
Addition
Subtraction

Appendix C: References for Parents and Tutors

All Kinds of Minds
24–32 Union Square East
6th Floor, Suite A
New York, NY 10003
Phone: 888–956-4637
Internet: *www.allkindsofminds.org*

Attention Deficit Disorder Association (ADDA)
15000 Commerce Parkway, Suite C
Mount Laurel, NJ 08054
Phone: 856–439-9099
Fax: 856–439-0525
Internet: *www.add.org*

Autism Society of America
7910 Woodmont Avenue, Suite 300
Bethesda, MD 20814–3067
Phone: 301–657-0881 or 1–800-3AUTISM (1–800-328-8476)
Internet: *www.autism-society.org/*

The Barbara Bush Foundation for Family Literacy
1201 15th Street NW, Suite 420
Washington, DC 20005
Phone: 202–955-6183
Fax: 202–955-5492
Internet: *www.barbarabushfoundation.com*

Bridges4Kids
3520 Okemos Road, Suite 6–150
Okemos, MI 48864
Phone: 1–877-HELP 4 KIDS (435-7454)
Internet: *www.bridges4kids.org*

Children with Attention Deficit Disorder (CHADD)
499 NW 70th Avenue
Suite 109
Plantation, FL 33317
Phone: 305–587-3700
Internet: *www.chadd.org*

The Council for Exceptional Children (CEC)
1110 North Glebe Road, Suite 300
Arlington, VA 22201
Voice phone: 703–620-3660
TTY: 866–915-5000
Fax: 703–264-9494
E-mail: service@cec.sped.org
Internet: *www.cec.sped.org*

Council for Learning Disabilities
11184 Antioch Road
Box 405
Overland Park, KS 66210
Phone: 913–491-1011
Fax: 913–491-1012
Internet: *www.cldinternational.org*

Federation for Children with Special Needs
1135 Tremont Street, Suite 420
Boston, MA 02120
Phone: 617–236-7210, 800–331-0688 (in MA)
Fax: 617–572-2094
Internet: *www.fcsn.org*

Institute on Disabilities
1301 Cecil B. Moore Avenue 423 Ritter Annex
Philadelphia, PA 19122
Voice/TTY: 215–204-1356
Fax: 215–204-6336
Internet: *www.temple.edu/instituteondisabilities/*

The International Dyslexia Association
40 York Road, 4th Floor
Baltimore, MD 21204–5202
Phone: 410–296-0232
Fax: 410–321-5069
Internet: www.interdys.org

International Reading Association
Headquarters Office
800 Barksdale Road
P.O. Box 8139
Newark, DE 19714–8139
Telephone: 1–800-336-READ (1–800-336-7323), United States and
Canada
Internet: *www.reading.org*

KU Center for Research on Learning
The University of Kansas
Center for Research on Learning
1122 West Campus Road, Room 521
Lawrence, KS 66045–3101
Internet: *www.ku-crl.org*

LD Online
Internet: *www.ldonline.org/*

Learning Disabilities Association of America
4156 Library Road
Pittsburgh, PA 15234–1349
Phone: 412–341-1515
Fax: 412–344-0224
Internet: *www.ldaamerica.org*

Learning Disabilities Worldwide, Inc.
P.O. Box 142
Weston, MA 02493
Phone: 781–890-LDWW (781–890-5399)
International Telephone: 001–781-890-LDWW (781–890-5399)
Fax: 781–890-0555
Internet: *www.ldworldwide.org*

MAAP Services for Autism and Asperger's Spectrum
P.O. 524
Crown Point, IN 46308
Phone: 219–662-1311
Fax: 219–662-0638
Internet: *www.asperger.org/MAAP*

National Autism Association (NAA)
1330 W. Schatz Lane
Nixa, MO 65714
Internet: *www.nationalautismassociation.org*

National Center for Learning Disabilities, Inc.
281 Park Avenue South
Suite 1420
New York, NY 10016
Phone: 212–545-7510
Internet: *www.ncld.org*

National Dissemination Center for Children with Disabilities
NICHCY
P.O. Box 1492
Washington, DC 20013
Voice/TTY: 1–800-695-0285
Voice/TTY: 202–884-8200
Fax: 202–884-8441
Internet: *www.nichcy.org*

National Institute of Child Health and Human Development
Building 31, Room 2A32
Bethesda, MD 20892–2425
Phone: 301–496-5133
Internet: *www.nichd.nih.gov/*

National Institute of Mental Health
Parklawn Building, Room 7C02
5600 Fishers Lane
Rockville, MD 20857–8030
Phone: 301–443-4515
Internet: *www.nimh.nih.gov/*

References

Alley, G., & D. Deshler, (1979). *Teaching the Learning Disabled Adolescent: Strategies and Methods.* Denver: Love.

Allsopp, D.H. (1997). Using classwide peer tutoring to teach beginning algebra problem-solving skills in heterogeneous classrooms. *Remedial and Special Education*, 18, 367–379.

Carman, R.H., & W.R., Adams, Jr. (1972). *Study Skills: A Student's Guide for Survival.* New York: Wiley.

Casale, U. (1985). Motor imaging: A reading-vocabulary strategy. *Journal of Reading*, 28, 619–621.

Englert, C.S., T.E. Raphael, & L. Anderson, (1985). *Teaching Cognitive Strategies to the Mildly Handicapped: A Classroom Intervention Study.* The Cognitive Strategy Instruction in Writing Project. Project funded by the U.S. Department of Education Office of Special Education Programs, East Lansing: Michigan State University.

Englert, C.S., & T.E. Raphael, (1988) Constructing well-formed prose: Process, structure, and metacognitive knowledge. *Research and Instruction in Written Language*, 54, 513–520.

Ives, B. & C. Hoy, (2003). Graphic organizers applied to higher-level secondary mathematics. *Learning Disabilities Research & Practice*, 18, 36–51.

Learning Disabilities Association of America, 2007.

LeBlanc, J.F. (1977). You can teach problem solving. *The Arithmetic Teacher*, 25, 16–20.

Maccini, P., & J.C. Gagnon, (2001). Preparing students with disabilities for algebra. *Teaching Exceptional Children*, 34, 8–15.

Maccini, P., & C.A. Hughes, (2000). Effects of a problem-solving strategy on the introductory algebra performance of secondary students with learning disabilities. *Learning Disabilities Research & Practice*, 15, 10–21.

Maccini, P., D. McNaughton, & K. Ruhl, (1999). Algebra instruction for students with learning disabilities: Implications from a research review. *Learning Disability Quarterly,* 22, 113–126.

Manalo, E., J.K. Bunnell, & J.A. Stillman, (2000). The use of process mnemonics in teaching students with mathematics learning disabilities. *Learning Disability Quarterly,* 23(2), 137–156.

Mason, L.H. (2004). Explicit self-regulated strategy development versus reciprocal question: Effect on expository reading comprehension among struggling readers. *Journal of Educational Psychology,* 96, 283–296.

Mason, L.H., K.H. Snyder, D.P. Sukhram, & Y. Kedem, (2006). TWA + PLANS strategies for expository reading and writing: Effects for nine fourth-grade students. *Exceptional Children,* 73, 69–89.

Mercer, C.D. (1994). Solving division equations: An algebra program for students with learning problems. Unpublished manuscript.

Mercer, C.D., L. Jordan, & S.P. Miller, (1996). Constructivistic math instruction for diverse learners. *Learning Disabilities Research & Practice,* 11, 147–156.

Mercer, C.D., & S.P. Miller, (1992). Teaching students with learning problems in math to acquire, understand, and apply basic math facts. *Remedial and Special Education,* 13, 19–35, 61.

National Reading Panel. (2000). *Teaching children to read: An evidence-based assessment of the scientific literature on reading and its implication for reading instruction.* NIH Publication No. 00–4769. Washington, DC: National Institute of Child Health and Development.

Pressley, M., J.R. Levin, & M.A. McDaniel, (1987). Remembering versus inferring what a word means: Mnemonic and contextual approaches. In M.G. McKeown & M.E. Curtis (eds.) *The Nature of Vocabulary Acquisition* (pp. 107–127). Hillsdale, NJ: Erlbaum.

Simmonds, E.P.M., J.P. Luchow, S. Kaminsky, & V. Cottone, (1989). Applying cognitive learning strategies in the classroom: A collaborative training institute. *Learning Disabilities Focus,* 4, 96–105.

Strichard, S.S, & C.T. Mangrum, II (1993). *Teaching Study Strategies to Students with Learning Disabilities.* Needham Heights, MA: Allyn & Bacon.

U.S. Department of Education. (1977). *P.L. 94–142. Federal Register,* Washington, DC, U.S. Government Printing Office, p. 65083.

Index